CW00410624

MANY
ARE THE
WONDERS

To

Becky

Still as beautiful

as ever!

inside and art.

love always

Deira x

MANY
ARE THE
WONDERS

DIANA WOOD

Michael Wood Publishing

Many Are The Wonders © 2021 Diana Wood.

The right of Diana Wood to be identified as the author of this work has been asserted by her in accordance with the Copyright, Designs, and Patents Act 1998

All rights reserved. No part of this publication may be reproduced, stored in a retrieval system, or transmitted in any other form or by any other means, electronic, mechanical, photocopying, recording or otherwise, without the prior permission of the publisher.

Cover Designed by Alexandra Hodgson

Scripture quotations taken from various Bible translations.

Author Name: Diana Wood

Visit my website at www.manyarethewonders.com.

First Printing: February 2021

Published by Michael Wood Publishing

Disclaimer: The publisher has no responsibility for the persistence or accuracy of URLs for external or third-party Internet websites referred to in this book, and does not guarantee that any content on such websites is, or will remain, accurate or appropriate.

British Library Cataloguing in Publication Data
A catalogue record for this book is available from the British Library.

ISBN: 9798700271813

Praise for

Many Are The Wonders

"Encouraging, uplifting, and sincere, the enthralling moments that Diana shares serve as a beautiful reminder that God is with us in all aspectsof our lives. To share in these special passages of time when He surrounds Diana and her family, shows that faith is the compass we need throughout life, a wonderful gift to us all. Diana is an inspiring and beautiful lady whose words shall warm the hearts of many."
Rebecca Andrew-Crowe, Author of *One Day at a Time*

"I've known Di Wood for twenty-plus years. I've always known her to be overflowing with love and compassion. This shines through the pages of her book, *Many Are the Wonders*. It's a book that will encourage, inspire, and bless you. I recommend this book. It will impart a resilience to keep on going forward with your eyes on Jesus, the author and perfecter of our faith."
Godfrey Birtill – Songwriter/Worship Leader

"This book is filled with amazing stories of faith. I remember the story of Diana and her daughter Alexandra attending my Spiritual Health Weekend when God spoke to them through my teaching on Eden. What a miraculous story of believing God for His promise. Diana has many stories like this – you must read this book. It will encourage you to trust God like never before."
Nancy Goudie – Author, Speaker, Founder of Nancy Goudie Ministries and Spiritual Health Weekends

"This book will bless and encourage you. Di is a living epistle; her faith is real and practical. If you want to read real stories of a God actively involved in a person's life, then this is a book for you."
Jack B. McVicar – Author and Co-Founder/Pastor, The Freedom Centre

"You will be captivated as you journey with Diana through her adventures of faith, as she stands upon God's word and just simply believes. This incredible woman is an inspiration and role model to a multitude, yet she walks humbly before her Lord and Saviour."
Rev. Bishop Ann Laidlow, Acorn International Ministries

"*Many Are the Wonders* by Di Wood is a word in season for all men and women who not only enjoy a good read, but who also enjoy reading of God's goodness, faithfulness, and love. Di is insightful and encouraging in proving that God works through our lives in the most mundane, day-to-day activities. Di draws from her own intimate relationship with her Lord and Saviour and from her 'Doctorate' from the 'University of Life'. Being a wife, a mother, and grandmother enables Di to write from her heart with deep emotion and empathy. Di writes of her own experiences with love, laughter, joy, and words that lead us closer to the heart of God. I wholeheartedly commend this book to one and all. It's an amazing read that guarantees a blessing."
Rev. Stephen Scholes, Retired Pastor

Dedication

I would like to dedicate this book to my amazing grandchildren who I love very much. To Isis, Shayla, Judah, Eden, Isaac, and Harriet. These stories are of how Nana saw God work and answer prayers in her life.

Scripture

Many, LORD my God, are the wonders you have done, the things you planned for us. None can compare with you; were I to speak and tell of your deeds, they would be too many to declare.

(Psalm 40:5 New International Version)

Acknowledgements

This book could not have happened without the help of so many people. I want to give a very special heartfelt appreciation and thanks to the following people.

Mark Swift, a Proofreader, Copy Editor and Indexer at Swift and Sure and a truly impressive, generous, and gifted young man. If you ever need anything proofreading, I can highly recommend Mark.

To my daughter Alexandra, I loved your book cover design and your lovely bio. You are so talented.

To ALL my children – Alexandra, Bobby, Lauren, Jennifer & Jacob. You are all amazing and without you many of the stories in this book simply wouldn't have happened. I love you all so much.

To Rebecca Andrew-Crowe, an author in her own right, a truly inspirational writer, and a beautiful woman inside and out.

To Jack McVicar, Nancy Goudie, Godfrey Birtle, Ann Laidlow, and Stephen Scholes for agreeing to read the initial manuscript and writing such lovely and encouraging words. God bless you all.

To all the friends and family who feature in these stories, including some who are no longer with us. I will be forever grateful for your love, encouragement, and inspiration.

To everyone who has given generously to help fund this book. We really couldn't have done it without you.

Last, but not least, to husband Mick, my biggest supporter, encourager, and the man I have chosen to spend my life with. Mick appears in a lot of the stories. Mick has also done a massive amount of the work needed to make this book come into being.

I am truly thankful to you all.

Lots of love, Diana xxx

CONTENTS

Introduction

The Apostle Paul was fruitful in his isolation times of being a prisoner and, even when he was in stinky prisons, he wrote letters to encourage and challenge the Churches in their faith walk. As we entered into a lockdown period of isolation due to the coronavirus, I decided that I wanted to put some positive posts onto Facebook. Especially at a time when people would be feeling frightened and fearful of the times we were all entering into.

I decided to write about some of the miracles and wonderful things that God had done personally for my family over the thirty-two years of knowing and loving Him. For years, I had wanted to write about these testimonies of God's goodness towards us as a family, but I had never got around to completing the book. As I wrote these short stories on Facebook, I didn't realise that I was now writing that book.

Many people had made comments on Facebook saying, "You need to write a book." The book before you now is the answer to those encouraging comments.

---

[1] The author, Diana Wood © Mick Wood, 2020

1

I wrote the stories which came to mind each day as I prayed and enquired of the Lord. Therefore, the stories are not in any particular chronological order and I have decided to leave them in the sequence that I was reminded of them.

The stories are quite short because they were originally written to be posted on Facebook. My prayer is that God will use these stories to speak to you and encourage you in your own faith walk with Him!

Trying to Keep Positive in the Midst of Crisis

That's what we all seem to be trying to do, as we are in unprecedented days. A couple of times last week, I had moments when my brain actually thought, This is all a bad dream and I am going to wake up soon. Even so, I am trying to just live one day at a time with hope in my heart and being thankful for every good thing that each day brings. From seeing my grandchildren on FaceTime to the joy of a good meal. We have had such lovely sunny weather to enjoy our daily walks with!

Yet, in the midst of all this, there are times of deep grief for the loss and the isolation of those who are dying from this despicable virus that has caused such carnage in our world. For the loss also of many things that we had taken for granted in our lives. There is the loss of the last days at school; the loss of not holding that brand-new baby that's just been born; the loss of not celebrating that planned big birthday with your family and friends; the loss of not being able to move to a new house. Deeper losses for those who can't get the surgery they were hoping for, but now have to wait, and some hope to live long enough

---

[2] Affirmations from Needpix.com / Public Domain, 2020

3

to see the day of that surgery! Yes, life has never quite looked like this before and it's very disconcerting, to say the least!

But yet I am still trying to dance in the rain. No one was more surprised than me when my husband said, "We are going to have a dance tonight in our lounge." God bless my treasure for trying to keep my spirits up in the midst of all this! He doesn't do dancing usually. In thirty-eight years of being together, we have probably danced three times, if that. Yes, I am literally going to dance in the storm and not wait for the storm to pass. We will all probably do those things with our precious loved ones, things that we should have been doing anyway.

Despite the grief of such devastating loss, and the very disturbing dreams when one sleeps, none of us have walked this way before, so take one step at a time, put one foot in front of the other, and if you start to wobble, then sit down for a while. Have a good cry, then get up and walk again, and try to dance in the rain with thankfulness in your heart as you walk!

Much love to you all in the midst of all this. Remember we are all in this together. Just trying to get through safely.

God bless you all, Diana

(Originally posted on 28th March 2020)

* This was the first day that I started to write on Facebook. As we went through lockdown to protect the country from the coronavirus, I was personally feeling a lot of grief over the loss of not being able to spend time with my family.

Family has always been the closest and dearest reason for my existence. After losing three people I dearly loved the year before, and still recovering from those losses, lockdown felt very cruel to me! I decided that I would try and do some positive actions during this difficult time.

I have always been one of those people that want good to come out of every situation. I personally believe that if we keep the right attitude, there will always be some good to be found in every difficulty that life throws at us!

4

And we know that God causes everything to work together for the good of those who love God and are called according to His purpose for them. **(Romans 8:28 – NLT)**

The Gift of Eden

I have been writing some memories in my journal this morning. One that stood out was my granddaughter's birth! The memory of how God told me and my daughter Alexandra that she would have a baby girl not long after Alexandra had suffered a miscarriage.

Alexandra and I attended a weekend Christian conference for women. The conference was run by an organisation called New Generation Music (NGM) which is headed up by a lady called Nancy Goudie. Nancy herself was the main speaker at the event.

3 Eden © Alexandra Hodgson, 2020

4

On the Friday evening, after arriving at the hotel in Garstang near Preston, both Alexandra and I had unpacked and settled into our rooms. We then headed off to the restaurant for our evening meal before going to the first session.

After the introduction and worship time, Nancy was the first speaker. It was during that evening meeting that I sensed God speaking to me through Nancy's message. The Lord told me that Alexandra would have a baby girl and she would be called Eden, which means 'pleasure and delight'. After hearing this word, I thought I would keep it in my heart and pray for confirmation.

The following morning, Alexandra came into the dining room and we had breakfast together. During the meal, Alexandra began to tell me that God had spoken to her the previous evening. I asked Alexandra, "What do you think God was saying to you?"

She went on to tell me that she believed that God was saying to her that she was going to have a baby, a little girl, and that she would be called Eden, which meant 'pleasure and delight'. I then went on to tell Alexandra that the Lord had said the exact same thing to me the previous evening, and that I had asked for confirmation.

This was in January 2013 and Eden was born on 19th November 2013. On the morning of the birth, at around 4 a.m., I got a call from Alexandra's husband James, telling me that it was time for me to come to the hospital as Alexandra was well into the labour. I got dressed and set off down the motorway to Royal Preston Hospital.

---

[4] Nancy Goudie © Nancy Goudie, 2020

When Eden finally came into this world, ten months after we had heard the Lord speak to us both, it was amazing! Eden came into the world so easily. One push and the head appeared, a second push and she was half out, a third push and Eden had been born within five minutes of the first push. After giving birth to three children myself, I knew this was an incredibly easy birth!

I held Eden in my arms as they sorted her mummy out after the birth. I was then able to declare over Eden, "You are amazing! You have even come into this world as a pleasure and delight!"

I couldn't stop kissing this amazing little child, a child that had truly lived up to the name that God had chosen for her. God has truly done so many wonderful and miraculous things over the years. I pray that they encourage and inspire you as you read about them.

God bless you all and keep you safe, Diana

(Originally posted on 4th April 2020)

[5] Alexandra and Eden © Alexandra Hodgson, 2015

A Gift of a Friend!

I remember a time when I was stuck at home with three little children. It was a time in our lives when my husband Mick was out all hours working two jobs. Mick has always been a good provider for our family and always worked hard! But for me, it was a very lonely time, especially when the children had gone to bed at 7 p.m.

I prayed that the Lord would provide a friend for me, someone who could drive so that they could come and see me at home when the kids were in bed. I also needed that friend to be single, so that she didn't need to be home in the evenings for her own husband. I was very specific in my prayers!

God sent into my life a woman that I had written a letter of encouragement to; her name was Maggie. When Maggie received the letter, she told me that she also needed a friend. She was a single parent whose daughters were now older teenagers busy living their own lives. Of course, this is the natural thing for teenagers to do. Maggie needed a friend, too. I was twenty-eight at that time and our friendship lasted eleven years. Then my dear friend Maggie died very suddenly.

---

[6] Maggie © Kat Ripley, 1998

During those years of friendship, we talked about everything. We didn't need to go to counselling or therapy, as our talking made us feel better. Maggie was a great support for me when Mick and I took on two more children after their mum had died from cancer. Our family grew from five to seven in a single day!

Without Maggie in my life at that time, I honestly don't know how I would have coped. Many tears were shed by both of us because Maggie had her own troubles to deal with, too!

The Bible says, "A friend loves at all times." **(Proverbs 17:17)**

Maggie was also a Sunday school teacher to one of my kids. I saw her nearly every day for a number of years. The song by Celine Dion, "Because You Loved Me", had some words in it that remind me of my faithful friend Maggie in those extremely difficult days:

> For all those times you stood by me
> For all the truth that you made me see
> For all the joy you brought to my life
> For all the wrong that you made right
> For every dream you made come true
> "For all the love I found in you,"

I'll be forever thankful, Maggie. You were the one who held me up and saw me through it all. My life was so very blessed because of you!

Maggie helped me to adjust to one of the most difficult challenges of my life, with her love and practical support.

If you have a truly good friend in your life, you are blessed beyond measure. Friends really are "the family we choose for ourselves"!

I am also truly blessed with friends that have walked life's path with me for more than half a lifetime. I have other friends who have joined me along this journey of life in my later years. I want you all to know I am truly blessed to have known the love of true friends, and that I am rich beyond measure with a life filled with the love of such friends!

My life is so very blessed because of you!

Thank the Lord for the gift of friendship!

(Originally posted on 5th April 2020)

[7] Di and Maggie © Kat Ripley, 1996

A Holiday in Devon

I remember when Mick was made redundant and was out of a job in the '90s. We had previously booked a holiday to Devon and paid for it when all was well, not knowing that job loss was coming. When Mick lost the job, we also lost the use of a company car.

We had no money to go on holiday and no car in which to travel. We were a young family and we never had any spare money in those days. We thought that we would have to cancel our holiday, realising that we also would not get any of our money back at that late date.

So, I decided to pray about the situation. As I prayed, I felt the Lord tell me to get everything ready to go. I ironed the family clothing and packed our suitcases. That was on the Monday evening and we were meant to be going on holiday on the Friday morning.

On the Wednesday evening of that week, we still had no money. In those days, we hosted a home group on Wednesday evenings, and at 10 p.m. on that particular Wednesday evening, I remember a friend – as she was leaving our home – giving me £15 and saying, "That's for your kids to get some ice creams on holiday." I said, "Thank you very much", but in my heart I was saying to God, *That's not going to get us very far, Lord.*

Three different families had offered to loan us their car, and one of them was a fancy new car with power steering, cruise control, and a CD player where you could load six CDs in the boot of the car. However, we literally had no money to put petrol in it. I prayed again, thinking this holiday might not happen, which was very frustrating when it had already been paid for.

By Friday morning, we had been given £278 in total from here, there, and everywhere! The petrol itself was going to cost around a hundred pounds to get us to Devon and back, and for us to also be able to travel around once we got there.

Anyway, we set off trusting God to help us with the holiday. We filled the car with petrol and off we went all the way down to Devon. I remember Mick saying that if we ran out of money, we would simply come home early.

When we arrived at the Haven Holidays site, we had been upgraded from a caravan to a bungalow-style chalet. The kids could go to the 'Tiger Club' and the beach was literally on camp – we were going to have a great time!

We went to church on the Sunday to thank the Lord for His provision and travelling mercies. We gave God a love offering out of our money to show Him how thankful we were.

On the Tuesday, as I sunbathed outside the chalet and the children were having a good time at the Tiger Club, I was reading my bible and felt the Lord say to me, *I am going to perform a miracle.* Shortly afterwards, a man came to post something to our chalet, which was strange, as nobody knew where we were. The camp was in the middle of nowhere, at the end of a long, dead-end country road with nothing else there. Inside the envelope, someone had written, "With love from Jesus." There was £50 in postal orders inside the envelope! How was this possible? As I mentioned earlier, **no one knew where we were!**

This gift from God meant that we could take our children for a good day out at the National Shire Horse Centre, which was just a short drive away! We had a very memorable day, which we all thoroughly enjoyed, and a very special holiday. We still have lovely photos of that holiday.

---

[8] National Shire Horse Centre © Mick Wood, 1992

Remember that **ALL** things are possible with God!

I hope you liked today's memory and stay safe, dear friends!

Love to you all, Diana

Many are the wonders that you have done oh Lord, if I were to tell of them there would be too many to mention! ***(Psalm 40:5)***

(Originally posted on 6th April 2020)

Stop Worrying

Today's memories are just a few of the things that the Lord has spoken into my heart in past struggles. I have been thinking that they may help someone else at this time.

There was a time in our family's life that we literally had to pray daily for everything, from children's shoes and uniforms, to bread and milk. I used to worry so much that it would make me physically ill. Remember that this was in the days before food banks were a thing.

I remember worrying about some bill that was due that we simply didn't have any money to pay. We hadn't even got to the day of payment and I was crying before the Lord about it in my bedroom, where the children wouldn't be able to see me. As I told the Lord all about it, I felt Him speak into my heart. *You can make yourself ill worrying about this for the next two weeks, or you can wait to see what I do in two weeks' time, and if I have not done something by that point, then you can worry.* By the time those two weeks were up, the situation had somehow been sorted!

Another time that I was worrying about not having food to feed my family, the Lord said to me, *Go and look in your cupboards; you have enough for today. I will sort out tomorrow when we get to it!* Lo and behold, when tomorrow came, I had the provision of food for my family.

I have realised that all of us can make ourselves upset and ill about things that haven't happened yet. I am currently learning that lesson again in these trying times! So, I say to us all today, including myself, these words from **Matthew 6:34**, "Do not worry about tomorrow, for tomorrow will bring its own worries. Today's trouble is enough for today!"

May God help protect your minds in these days and strengthen us all in the challenges that we all face. May He also provide for your needs in miraculous ways! Love to you all and stay safe, dear ones, because you are very loved and precious to me and the Lord.

Take care, Diana

(Originally posted on 7th April 2020)

The Storm

Today, I have decided to share one of my poems on my post. It is a poem that I wrote during some very difficult years of my life.

I was having my own serious health issues at that time and I was in and out of hospital for biopsies every six months for three years.

During that time, my son and my daughter went through breakdowns one after the other. My dad and sister were also ill.

If I wrote any more, you would think it sounded like a bad soap opera, but it really was just too ridiculous to be true. Anyway, I am still here to tell the tale.

Here is the poem written by me, inspired by that time!

THE STORM
Wave after wave crashed over my soul,
Hitting my life with many cruel blows.
Over and over from the left and the right,

---

[9] Photograph from PxHere.com, 2020

Until I felt that I was losing my sight.
My faith and trust in God alone was being eroded,
as He watched from His throne!
God had warned me beforehand, *A time of trial is to come,*
He wasn't surprised by what was happening, but I called on His son.
My anchor held within the veil,
through the storms of life I was endeavouring to sail.
Sometimes it felt like all hope was gone,
but my faith in God was what I had built my life upon!
Then I remembered His promise, *This too will pass,*
The storm went on so long, I thought it would surely last.
God's word says, *Weeping remains for a night but joy comes in the morning,*
Trusting in these words would send my spirit soaring!
On and on the waves seemed to roll,
The storm kept coming and on Jesus I would call!
The storm lasted years, seemed like it would never end,
In the midst of it all I even lost a few friends.
Some friends stay only in fair weather,
But true friends stick with you in good and bad times forever!
Never will God leave me or forsake me I am told,
The truth of that word never grows old!
The storm has gone still now or so it seems,
God has given me some amazing new dreams.
Dreams that have come true and a guaranteed happy ending,
My precious God in heaven His love He is sending;
And piece by piece my soul He's restoring and mending!
As for the future? I am trusting it to God,
On whom I am depending!

Remember my friends, "**THIS TOO WILL PASS!**"

Keep safe, I love you all, Diana

(Originally posted on 8th April 2020)

Good Friday

Sometimes, people ask, "Why is it called Good Friday when it's when Jesus died a horrific death on a cross over 2,000 years ago?"

Here is a poem I wrote many years ago.

THERE WAS A MAN

There was a man who came to earth,
A tiny babe of humble birth.
People thought he was just a carpenter's son,
They didn't know he had come to Earth for God's will to be done.
He came to live a life completely free from sin,
That we might come to know and love him.

He performed many miracles in three and a half years,
He was full of compassion and even shed tears.
His friends all loved him – all but one,
Through his act of betrayal it was done.

Thirty pieces of silver was the price of the deed,
Sold to his enemies that he may meet our need.
God laid on him the sins of everyone,
So that His precious children we could become.

To prison and to trial they led him away to be,
Oppressed and afflicted for you and for me.
Cursed at and accused, he never said a word.
Yet as they nailed him to a cross this is what they heard.

"Father forgive them, for they know not what they do,"
He even defended them as he took the punishment for you!
Poured out his life unto death – God's will had been done.
As for the world – a new day had begun!

Take care, Diana

(Originally posted on 10th April 2020)

A Miracle for Debbie

Today, I want to tell you about a time in 2016 when it looked like my sister Deborah – or as I preferred to call her, Debbie – was dying. She was too poorly to be operated on; her only chance was a miracle from God!

She had a massive blood clot in her tummy, and she was bleeding internally, caused by a hospital investigatory procedure. My husband and I drove over to be with Debbie. When we arrived at Deb's bedside, some of her family were already there.

The family had gathered around her hospital bed at Aintree Hospital. I whispered in her ear, "Deborah Keaveney, you shall not die, but live, and declare the works of the Lord," my words inspired by **Psalm 118:17**.

My mum was crying, and others, too, but as I prayed for my sister, I felt peace. I stayed a while, wondering, *Do I stay, or do I go home? Is this going to be the end?* I honestly did not know what to do.

I decided that I would go home because I felt peace for Deb. Then I said, "I am going to go now." Deb's husband Patrick called me over to him and said quietly, "You do know that things can turn around in an hour?"

I realised that if I went home, I wouldn't get back to the hospital in time if Deb was about to die. I thought about it and thought, *I have peace; I have done what I came to do, which was to pray with my sister.* I turned around and said to Deb, "I will see you in the morning, Deb." As I walked away from her bed, I really believed that I would!

That evening, at around 10 p.m., I heard God say to me, *Only believe and you will see.*

What will I see, Lord?

Only believe and you will see the glory of God!

This word gave me such faith! But this faith thing was not going to be a one prayer miracle! At times, I would think that Deb's life was coming to an end!

Deb was in hospital for seven weeks. She went from bad to worse, one thing after another. On top of the blood clot that they couldn't operate on, she got pneumonia and shingles. They had to stop giving her a drip at one point, because this was also causing problems. With every new obstacle, we had to pray. We took John Kiseba, a mighty man of God from Zambia, to pray for Deb in hospital.

Before Deb was taken so ill, she had organised for someone to come and build a play area in a corner of her very large garden. She had not been well for a few years before this, and she wanted somewhere she could watch her grandchildren play, because she couldn't take them to the park.

I prayed with all my heart that Deb would get to see those grandchildren play in her garden. She got such joy from her grandchildren – they kept her going during many years of battling illness!

There were times in those seven weeks that I just said to God, *Take her home if she's going to have to suffer so much.*

But God had said, and He doesn't go back on His word. I believed easily at the beginning but, when everything seemed against Deb coming out of hospital, I did at moments start to believe instead in the circumstances.

I am glad that my faith in God doesn't depend on me and my wobbly moments, but instead on who He is and what He says!

Seven weeks later, my beautiful sister came home from hospital. She lived for another three years after that, and she got to see her grandchildren play in that fabulous play area for many happy days!

She has gone to be with the Lord now and I miss her every single day. I am left with three extra years of wonderful memories, where Deb got to see another granddaughter born and her daughter Christine married in her beautiful garden, and many other wonderful, treasured memories.

I thank God on this resurrection weekend, that I got to experience God's resurrection power at work in my sister's life!

> Then Jesus said, "Did I not tell you that if you believe, you will see the glory of God?" **(John 11:40)**

Take care, Diana

(Originally posted on 11th April 2015)

---

[10] Di with her sister Debbie on a Norwegian cruise in June 2015 © Diana Wood, 2015

The Inspirational Letter

Often times, God gives us one piece of the jigsaw to move forward with, just like Abraham in the Bible in Genesis 12:1. Here is one such story from me. I honestly didn't know what to write today until I was reminded of this verse!

In the year 2000, I decided I wanted to do something special for a charity that I served for over twenty years called *The Harvesters Trust*. My friend Carol had sent me a letter of encouragement, and in the letter, she inspired me with her words. She told me that the two extra children that God had given us in 1995 were just a seed of what God wanted to do for orphans!

I decided, because of that letter, that I would set myself a goal of raising £10,000. I was so scared, because I had never raised that amount of money for one project for the charity before that point. Once I had made that decision, I felt God say to me, *You will exceed that amount, but others will help you!*

My first piece of the jigsaw was to swim a mile, to literally go the extra mile like it talks about in the Bible **(Matthew 5:41)**. I set off, training to swim that mile with my friend Carol, who was going to help me raise that money. We swam the mile and raised around £400 between us.

We were doing lots of other little things as well. For example, cake sales, car boot sales, and sponsored walks. However, we were still such a long way off the goal.

A man approached me and said that he would like to do a sponsored bike ride to Romania to raise money for the orphanage. He, together with a small team of other men, raised over £3,500 towards the goal.

Then a lady, who was one of our neighbours and who had recently become a Christian, wanted to run in the New York City Marathon to raise money for the orphanage, too. She took a team across to America and they raised £7,000 in total. We had now raised just under £11,000, enough to build the orphanage!

That year, I met a missionary who knew about a team in America who were waiting for the funds so that they could build an orphanage in Zambia.

My piece of the jigsaw was to raise the money with others helping me. Who would do that? I had no idea, but God engineered it all. The missionary man's vision was to build the orphanage! Isn't it amazing how God brings all the pieces of the jigsaw together?

In the year 2001, the beginning of October to be exact, the 'Refreshed Pot Care House' was completed and officially opened by our missionary friends John and Kathy Potter. The orphanage was home for up to eighty children.

11

Whatever piece of the jigsaw God gives you, just do it! You will be amazed at how He arranges all the other pieces to complete it!

May God continue to bless you all with good health and keep you safe.

Take care, love Diana

(Originally posted on 13th April 2020)

---

11 John Potter and some of the orphans. Refreshed Pot Care House, Kafue, Zambia © Mick Wood, 2004

The Flour Jar

I remember when my husband Mick was thinking about becoming self-employed, leaving his regular job to do that. With three young children at that time, I was afraid for our future. Would we have enough money to manage on?

Mick asked me to pray about it before he made his final decision. I decided to get up very early the next morning, before the kids woke up, to seek God.

My daily reading that morning was all about the widow of Zarephath. The verse **1 Kings 17:14** in particular really spoke to me:

> For this is what the LORD, the God of Israel, says: "The jar of flour will not be used up and the jug of oil will not run dry until the day the LORD sends rain on the land."

In those days, I had a big glass jar on the kitchen counter. It was filled with flour, as I was always baking. I felt God speak into my spirit, *I will always hear you scraping the bottom of the flour jar.*

I cannot tell you how many times over the years people just turned up to my house and said, "I just felt to bring you some flour." Some of those times I had literally just used up my last flour to bake for other people.

Sometimes, they would come bringing me flour not knowing I had made cakes for them to take home. Over the years, the flour jar was always a constant of God's provision and faithfulness to our family!

In these coronavirus days, when flour has been difficult to get hold of, I still have flour and cakes to give away. It reminds me that God is not the God of just getting by, but the God of having enough!

The God whose generosity OVERFLOWS! I need not worry about the future, but trust in a God who has more than taken care of us over the years.

And many of your friends out there will remember stories such as these!

God bless you all and keep you safe and protected in these very sad days.

> *I do not know what the future holds, but this I do know!*
> *I am held by the one who knows my future!* – Ralph Abernathy

Take care, love Diana

(Originally posted on 14th April 2020)

Life Begins at Forty!

No, I know that life doesn't begin at forty, but it's an old saying. I was aged forty when I sensed God calling me to go on a mission trip to Russia. Before then, I had never even been on an aeroplane, and I had felt no desire to leave our beautiful country.

I had five children, some of whom were still at school. I didn't want to leave them for the length of time the mission would take. Two weeks is a long time, especially as I had never left them for more than two nights before this.

I knew God was speaking and I couldn't pretend that I hadn't heard Him. Therefore, I had to rise to the challenge, even though the thought of going on a plane made me panic inside.

I remember crying on my bed two nights before I was due to travel. I was thinking and praying, *I just cannot do this, Lord, please help me!* I was scared that I would have a panic attack on the plane. I had one once before, just because I had stepped onto a coach and they had closed the door behind me.

Off I went in obedience to Manchester Airport on 1st October 2002 – I was now forty-one years old. I went with our mission team leader to park the car and I remember watching the planes coming in to land every five minutes or so and giving myself a mental pep talk.

The planes are landing here every five mins. How often do you actually hear of a plane crash? Now get a grip, girl!

We stayed in a hotel that night and got up very early to get our flight. Firstly, we went from Manchester to Paris, France. We landed there to get our next flight to St Petersburg, Russia. I was absolutely ecstatic when I got off the plane at Paris Charles de Gaulle Airport. People around me must have thought that I was drunk, as I was singing this God song out loud:

> SOMEDAY THEY'LL HEAR THE TRUMPET,
> SOMEDAY THEY'LL HEAR THE SOUND,
> WHEN THE STRONG NAME OF YOU, LORD JESUS,
> WILL BE WORSHIPPED IN EVERY LAND!

May I tell you that I was loud!

We were ushered through the airport by staff because our first plane had been delayed, but my joy remained. We arrived safely in Russia after experiencing turbulence for the first time. I remember feeling fear as I arrived there, and it attacked me for a few days.

On the journey from St Petersburg to Pskov, we broke down at the side of the road. I honestly thought that my husband would get an email telling him that I had frozen to death at the side of the road.

A few things happened that instilled that fear in me, but after someone prayed with me a few days into the mission, fear or anxiety became no longer a problem in my life. I am not saying I don't have moments, but they don't hang around!

We had a very successful mission in Russia. We visited hospitals, taking equipment to them. We visited orphanages, taking yoghurts and bananas in for the children. We also spoke at women's conferences in every town that we visited.

[12] Pskov Hospital, Russia © Diana Wood, 2002

I was asked to preach to the youth and gave testimonies in meetings and churches as we travelled around Russia. It was a heart-breaking and emotional mission, but it was also life-changing for me!

Since that first trip in 2002, I have travelled on aeroplanes many times; some of those journeys I have travelled alone. It gives me a joy and excitement when I travel that always feels like I'm going on a *God adventure*!

> I can do all this through him who gives me strength. **(Philippians 4:13)**

Take care, love Diana

(Originally posted on 15th April 2020)

---

[13] Ostrov Bridge, Russia © Diana Wood, 2002

My Beloved

Today, I didn't know what to write, but then I remembered this poem that I wrote many years back. Then I thought, *No, I can't put that online.* This evening, my friend sent me a card which included a reference to the same passage in the Bible that originally inspired my poem.

I took this as a confirmation so here is the poem.

MY BELOVED

> The love of my life is like no one that I have ever known before.
> When I awake in the morning and see the sun rising, I think of Him.
> When I look up into the night sky and see the stars and moon shining brightly, I think of Him.
> He is brighter than the sun or any shining star.
> His beauty, far more lovely than the most beautiful of flowers.
> His purity, whiter than the whitest snow; so white I cannot look upon Him!
> When I sense Him close to me, I feel more beautiful and loved than anyone else on Earth.
> It seems that His love is so consuming, that there couldn't be any love left over for anyone else.

---

[14] © Mick Wood, 2020

Yet He loves you just the same as me.
The love that He shows towards me in all its depth and purity:
He has also for you!
His hands are constantly outstretched towards you;
they still bear the nail marks where He was pierced for you.
The love He has for me is there also for you;
If only you would accept it?

Take care, love Diana

(Originally posted on 16th April 2020)

A Healing for Mick

Today, I want to tell you about a story that came to mind this morning. I remember the time when we had just taken on two more children. Their mummy had sadly died of cancer at the age of twenty-eight. God entrusted her two precious children to us.

Why do I say God? Because He spoke to me three weeks before their mummy died and said, *I am giving these children to you; they are a blessing and an inheritance. They are not a burden and not to be viewed as such!*

15

It was about six months after taking the children into our home that Mick, my husband, got ill. He kept having lots of nose bleeds and the doctors discovered that he had a growth in his face which they thought was cancerous.

It was the Thursday before Good Friday and Mick had a hospital appointment with a specialist. The doctor said to Mick that he had a one-in-four chance of dying. Mick took ages coming back from the hospital. I thought that something was very wrong but didn't know what it was.

---

[15] Jacob and Jennifer © Mick Wood, 1995

When Mick finally came home, I was devastated by his news. I was beginning to think that I was going to be left alone with five children to bring up on my own.

God knew better and we prayed together that this growth would shrink, and the cancer would go. The doctor had said "It looks angry," so we prayed that whatever it was would calm down. Two weeks later, we went to see the specialist again and he told us that, "The growth seems to have shrunk and it doesn't seem as angry."

The doctor asked us to come back again in two weeks' time and he told us that he would then decide on whether to operate or not. We continued to pray, believing that God had already begun to work on the situation.

Two weeks later, we returned to see the specialist and he told us that the growth had **completely disappeared!** God had heard our prayers and performed a miracle! There was no operation needed.

How good and kind God was to us! And still is, might I add!

Keep safe, dear ones. I hope this story encourages your faith in Jesus. After all, "nothing is impossible with Him"! **(Luke 1:37)**

Take care, love Diana

(Originally posted on 21st April 2020)

Crossing Over the River! – Part One

I remember towards the end of the year 2000, Mick and I sensed that God was bringing about a massive shift in our lives. We felt that God was calling us to move to St Annes, across the River Ribble. We had been going to share the vision of the charity that Mick had founded to a few churches on the Fylde coast for a few years, but never dreamed that one day we would live there.

16

Some friends of ours who lived in St Annes were going to go to Bible college and they asked us if we wanted to rent their house whist they were away. We said "Yes" because at that time we were sensing God's call to move to St Annes.

At that time, we were pastoring a small church in Chorley, but we knew that it was time to lay down all the wonderful works that we were doing – we were certain of that!

The house that we were going to live in was too beautiful for words. It would have been a dream to live there compared to bringing five children up in a three-up, two-down terraced house in Chorley. The house in Chorley was a happy home, but we needed more space as the children were all growing up.

---

16 Andrew Mathewson / River Ribble – https://creativecommons.org/licenses/by-sa/4.0/

I was sad to be leaving my support system of our church and friends behind, although very happy that we were sensing and responding to God's call in our lives.

It got to around halfway through 2001 and I went to visit the friends whose house we were going to rent. Whilst I was there, I sensed that the house was flying away, like a butterfly from my hand.

Then, not long afterwards, our friends told us that they needed to sell the house rather than rent it out. There was no way we could have afforded to buy that house, but I also felt that maybe it wasn't meant to be? We started to look for a property that we could rent by September 2001, in time for the school year starting.

For the money that we could afford, the properties in St Annes were not fit to take our family into. I said to the Lord that, if it was just Mick and I, then we would go anywhere, but I wasn't going to take our family into a worse situation than the one we were already living in.

We organised a joint fortieth birthday party at the end of July 2001. It was also to be our 'goodbye to Chorley' party. We had a special time celebrating with 200 of our family and friends, yet still we had no home to live in, and September was getting very close.

Someone had given Mick and I a gift for our birthdays. It was a break to Arnside near Silverdale. Whilst we were there, on the Friday before we went home, we went to pray on a beach. We cried out to the Lord that we believed He wanted us to move but doors were appearing to close. We really cried out to Him in desperation. When we returned home that evening, someone had left a message on our answering machine.

The message was left by our new pastor's wife (we had already started to travel across to the church where we were hoping to settle). She said to us, "The house next door to us is going to be rented out, are you interested in coming to see it?"

It had four bedrooms, two bathrooms, two living rooms, a dining room, and a kitchen, spread across three floors. There was also a cellar. In summary, it was ideal for a big family! Unfortunately, we had no money for a deposit or enough furniture to fill such a large house, but that will be tomorrow's story!

Take care, love Diana

TO BE CONTINUED

(Originally posted on 22nd April 2020)

Crossing Over the River! – Part Two

When we went to view the house in St Annes, we loved it. It had so much space for our large family.

Mick and I had come to an agreement before we went to view the house as to how much we could stretch our faith to for the rent. The landlord wanted exactly that amount of money and, to be honest, the house was worth around £200 more a month in rent than he was asking for.He also wanted to leave some furniture in the house rather than putting it into storage. That fitted in brilliantly with us, because we didn't have enough furniture for such a big house.

Earlier on that year, I had sensed God telling me to write a wish list in my journal, which I still have as you can see in the image below. One of the things on the wish list for my new house that had yet to arrive was a bed settee, so that we could have visitors stay in our seaside town house.

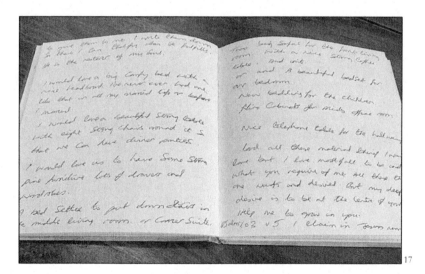

17

---

[17] Di's journal, 29th April 2001 © Diana Wood, 2020

The furniture left in the house consisted of a brand-new three-piece suite with two settees – one of which was a bed settee – one very large armchair, a big oak table with strong chairs, and brand-new beds and good wardrobes upstairs.

These were items of furniture that we simply didn't have the money to buy at that time, because Mick had been studying at university for the previous few years and it had seriously been worse than being on benefits. We couldn't even get free school meals for our kids, or prescriptions paid for.

It was early on a Thursday evening in August, at around 9 p.m., when we set off home to Chorley after viewing the house. We had already said to the homeowner that we wanted the house, even though we had no money for the deposit. In total, we needed to find £1,100, which was – and still is – a lot of money when you have no savings.

Mick decided that he was going to see our bank manager and try and get a loan for the deposit. I said, "I think that we should pray and ask God to help us." That's exactly what we did. We prayed for £1,000 (we had already put aside £100) and said to the Lord that it could come in dribs and drabs from wherever He wanted it to come from.

On the Sunday morning, we travelled across from Chorley and went to church in St Annes. A missionary couple came up to us and gave us an envelope, telling us that the Lord had told them to give it to us. Inside the envelope was a cheque for £1,000! Wow! God never ceased to amaze us in His provision and His loving kindness towards us, and in the way that He took care of us!

The furniture that we had from our house in Chorley fitted into the second lounge and we therefore had all that we needed for the house. My wish list was completed in every way!

We lived in that house for seven years. The landlord never once put the rent up and the Lord took care of us in many ways. He even provided a job for me in a Christian café that fit in with the children's schooling to help pay the rent. He also provided places in local schools for our children, places that we had to appeal and fight for once we had moved there. The Lord did it all and even more than that!

I hope this story encourages you to take your prayers and your impossible situations to the Lord. You just never know what He will do to help you!

Take care, love Diana

(Originally posted on 23rd April 2020)

Satan Has Asked That You Be Sifted Like Wheat

I remember when, approximately eight years ago, I was exercising in Mick's office on the cross trainer. I used to put worship music on and many times the Lord would speak to me as I exercised. One particular day, God spoke to me and said, *Satan has asked that you be sifted like wheat.* (Luke 22:31) I sat down immediately, wondering what on earth was coming upon my life.

A time of great trials was about to begin in my life that lasted many years. God was with me and God brought me through! Every difficulty comes to pass, and seasons change.

Within a few weeks of hearing the Lord warn me about the trials, I was going into hospital for a biopsy procedure. The specialist had discovered that I had a condition in my womb that could turn into cancer.

Every six months, for the rest of my life, I would have to undergo a minor operation for this biopsy. Or, so the doctors said.

Thank God that He has the final say about what happens in our lives!

---

[18] © Mick Wood, 2020

As I sought the Lord about this, I believed that He would heal me, but my own thoughts would say, *Is that you just believing or is God really going to heal you?*

Every six months for three and a half years, I would go into hospital as a day patient for a biopsy and camera procedure to see if the condition had progressed. I got to the point where I had had enough of it all. I couldn't imagine going into hospital like that for the rest of my life.

I told the Lord that I had had enough of it all. My airways had collapsed during one of the ops and I was aware of the dangers, even if it was just a minor op.

The last two biopsies were clear. They were taken six months apart and showed that the condition, which the doctors had told me wasn't curable, was no longer affecting me. The doctors said at my last hospital appointment that I no longer needed to go in for any more ops, because those last two biopsies had been clear.

I was only to go back and see the specialist if any more symptoms occurred. Well, my friends, I am still here, symptom-free, five years down the road!

God says in His word that He will not let us be tempted beyond what we can bear. He will give us a way out. God made a way for me where there seemed to be no way.

By the way, during those years, many other difficulties and trials were also happening in my life, but God brought me through them all.

Remember this, dear friends. Whatever life brings, it all comes to pass; nothing stays forever! Hold on to hope, for hope will never disappoint you!

God bless you all.

Take care, love Diana

(Originally posted on 24th April 2020)

The Retreat

I thought that I would share one of my poems again today, as I have been sharing some of the amazing testimonies about the goodness of God in my life over the last few weeks.

I remember once being on a retreat and a man was teaching stuff I didn't believe about evolution. I just thought to myself, *He's probably read too many clever books that he can't just have faith in God's word.* He was going to do a service in the chapel at the retreat centre. Because of some of his strange teaching, I didn't know if I wanted to listen to him again. I was sat in the chapel telling the Lord what His word said to Him about creation and other things.

Then, when this man began to preach, he spoke on the words Jesus said to Peter, "Who do you say I am?" **(Matthew 16:16–20)** Through His word, I heard the Lord saying to me, *Who do you say I am, Diana?* This was my reply in poem form:

WHO IS HE TO ME?

    Who is He to me?
    Now let me see.
    Who is He to me?
    The king for all eternity, the Christ, the son of God,
    the one who sets me free!
    He's creator and redeemer, everything that's good and true.
    The Alpha and Omega, the one who makes all things new.
    My king, my Lord, my saviour, and my closest friend;
    He's the lover of my soul from the beginning to the end.
    He's the one who has written my name on the palms of His hands.
    Let me tell you, my friends, I'm His number one fan!
    He's the one who holds me close to His heart.
    Nobody and nothing will pull this love apart!
    He's the restorer of my soul, healer, and deliverer, too.
    May I ask you a question?
    "Who is He to you?"

Take care, love Diana

(Originally posted on 25th April 2020)

Six New Windows

I remember in 1996, the year after we had been given two more children from the Lord, that Mick had been out of work with depression for almost two years and our little terraced house in Chorley needed some vital repairs.

In particular, the boys' bedroom window was rotting and there was now a hole with air and sometimes rain coming through it. Our youngest son had asthma and was not really able to sleep in that room as it was.

We had no money to get a new window and, besides, the house would look kind of strange with just one new window. A new bypass opened up at the side of our house and we managed to get some compensation from the council to help with soundproofing, because of the increased traffic noise.

The council put in a new soundproofed back door and also gave us an amount of money to help get double-glazed windows to help shut out the noise of the traffic. The money that they gave us, plus some money that was given as a gift from Leyland Pentecostal Church when we first took on the children, helped us to scrape together enough money for three new windows. A missionary couple who had just returned from Africa and started a business were employed to do the work for us.

The windows arrived and were placed in our backyard, waiting for the workers to come and fit them in the next day. Mick must have been out somewhere when they were delivered. I remember saying to him when he got home, "Mick, you know our double-glazed windows, do they put one window on the inside and one on the outside? Because there are six windows out in the yard."

Mick said, "Don't be silly."

I said, "Well, you had better take a look in the yard."

Mick had a look in the yard and realised that six windows had indeed been delivered. He got on the telephone to the contractor and told him there had been a mistake. The ex-missionary guy told us, "There is no mistake."

Without us knowing anything about it, this man had phoned around some of our friends and had raised enough money to have the whole of the house fitted with new double-glazed windows!

The workmen who came to fit the windows did the work for free! They also brought with them new quilts, with covers for them, and lots of other nice things for the kids' bedrooms. We were totally overwhelmed by their kindness and generosity!

[19] New windows – 20 Oxford Street, Chorley © Mick Wood, 2020

Yet again, God had performed a miracle as far as we were concerned. The miracle of God's people coming together to do an incredible act of kindness for a young family that was struggling to cope. As I have said before:

Many are the wonders that you have done for us, oh Lord. If we were to tell of them, there would be too many to count! **(Psalm 40:5)**

I do not understand why God has always been so good to us. This is a mystery, but one thing that I know for sure is that His goodness and mercy has surrounded our lives!

Stay safe and know that God loves you, too, and wants to help you in whatever situation you are facing.

Why not ask the Lord Jesus if He will help you, too? You may well be amazed by the answer to the prayer, just like I was.

Take care, love Diana

(Originally posted on 27th April 2020)

An Hour With Dad – The Gift of Time Outside a Window!

On Sunday morning, I travelled across to see my dad at his care home. Because of the coronavirus, we had not been allowed to visit him for weeks. We had managed to have some telephone calls with him, but no actual visits for about two months.

The home had contacted my brother, who then informed me that my dad was not well; in fact, he may have had the coronavirus. I just thought that it could be some other virus. My dad had suffered from ill health in other areas, so I knew that any illness could take him.

Anyway, I phoned the care home up and asked if I could see my dad through his window and would they open the window so that I could speak to him? They said that would be OK and yes, I could bring along some of his favourite foods. I felt that it would give my dad hope and help him to fight.

We set off down the motorway on the Sunday morning to spend time at his window, not knowing the gift that God was giving me in this!

When I got there, I telephoned the care home to let them know that I was outside the building as arranged. The nurse in charge of my dad wasn't around, so I asked the reception to inform the nurse Marieshelle that I was there, and I would be outside my dad's window.

The care home is built on one level like a bungalow, so I walked around the perimeter to my dad's window. When I got to it, I found that the curtains were closed but that the window was slightly open.

Marieshelle was nowhere to be seen and I didn't want to wait. I managed to get my hand through a small gap in the window and yanked the curtain back strongly so that it would open. I could see my dad and began to shout to him through the window. He must have been so shocked to hear my voice, but he began to speak back to me and respond.

I had asked my children to send me messages of love to speak out to him at the window. I had also asked my daughter to send a version of the song "Amazing Grace" to play on my telephone to him through the window. Marieshelle arrived and opened the curtain even further back, so that the room was lighter and I could see my dad more clearly.

I spent an hour at the window relaying the messages of love that everyone had sent for him. I played Susan Boyle's version of "Amazing Grace" and even tried to sing along but couldn't for crying.

Then Mick came to the window and my dad saw him and waved. He always loved Mick and was really happy to see him. It was very timely as I could stop crying while Mick interacted with him. Mick said "Goodbye" and I carried on talking to my dad at the window for as long as I could. I watched him eat his cheese sandwich and a scone that I had made for him that morning. Then I telephoned the duty nurse to come in to help my dad before I left.

I told my dad that I would come to see him soon at the window again and that my brother would come and see him at the window the following day. I felt that I had given him hope to fight and I told him we would soon be able to visit him properly when the lockdown was over.

[20]

I told him I loved him and said "Goodbye", not realising that my dad would die early the next morning, before my brother got to see him at the window. The

---

[20] Diana and her dad in St Annes © Mick Wood, 2016

Lord had given me literally a gift of a window to say goodbye to my dad. I got to see my lovely dad during the lockdown.

I had thought that I was taking my dad hope, but I was given a special gift that was far more valuable! At a time that has brought such sadness, such loss of contact, and such loss of friends and family members in our world, God gave me that gift of time and a window that I am so very thankful for!

Why? Because many others in the middle of this pandemic have not received such a gift! My sweet and lovely dad died early the following morning. I was in utter shock! I had not realised that Dad was so near to death. If I had realised, I don't know if I would have left that window.

The following morning, Mick put a post on Facebook:

So yesterday Diana's dad died. He had been unwell for a while but kept his faculties right up to the end. He wasn't in pain and we got to see him the day before when we were able to talk to him through a partially open window at his care home. I have known Brian for forty years and he was always kind to me. He will be missed but my faith means that I'll see him again one day.

Please keep telling your friends and family that you love them – one day you won't be able to!

Take care, love Diana

(Originally posted on 28th April 2020)

A Little Boy's Prayer

I remember a time when we went out in our car up to the hills just outside Chorley. All of our five kids squashed up on the back seat of the car. This was in the days before kids' special booster seats or car seats were commonplace. We realised that the kids were growing fast and we couldn't keep fitting them in the car like that.

We went to Anglezarke, a place of beauty just outside Chorley. It was there that our son Bobby prayed that God would provide an eight-seater car for us all. He had heard me telling his dad that, "We can't continue to squash the kids up on that back seat anymore."

Not long after that, I remember walking past an eight-seater car and saying to the Lord, *One just like that will do, Lord!* I had no idea that this was to be the very car that would be the answer to a little boy's prayer!

We had started going as a family to Chapel House Church in Chorley. A family that was as big as ours also went to the same church. It was quite unusual to have such a big family in those days and it's even more unusual now.

21

The mum of that same family asked me to go out for coffee one day and came to pick me up in the very same car that I had mentioned to the Lord. I'd had no

---

21 This was the model – an 8-seater, 5-door 2.0 Toyota Space Cruiser © Mick Wood, 2020

idea that it belonged to that family when I prayed to the Lord. The car was an eight-seater Toyota Space Cruiser with a window that opened in the roof. In fact, it was a car way above our limited means.

As we drank our coffees, I happened to say to the woman who owned the car, "If ever you want to sell your car, please will you let me know, as we really need a bigger car for our growing family."

She answered me right away and said, "We are waiting on a new car being delivered and it has been delayed for some reason." Unfortunately, her husband didn't really like to sell things to people he knew in case something went wrong.

I went home and prayed about it, knowing that, whatever the man usually did, if God wanted us to buy that car, then it would open up to us! To be honest, we didn't even have money to buy the car, but I knew that we needed one and we had been praying. If they did change their minds and decide that they would be willing to sell us the car, then I would simply pray the money in, as I had done so many times before for our needs.

One Sunday after church, we were stopped by the woman who said, "My husband is willing to sell the car to you."

I asked her, "How much do you want for the car?"

She told me, "I will get my husband to ring you about it." Now we needed to find out the cost and pray the money in!

When her husband phoned up later that day, he asked my husband Mick what our car was worth and Mick said it was worth maybe £500. The man said that, "The price of my car is whatever money you get when you sell your car."

Wow! We didn't expect that. Mick told the man, "Our car is only worth a few hundred pounds and your car is obviously worth a whole lot more than ours!"

The man insisted again, "The price of the car is whatever, and I mean whatever, price you get for your car!"

Unfortunately, our car developed a problem and so the estimate of £500 turned out to be too much – it was worth even less than £500, while the Space Cruiser was worth more than £1,000. So, Mick wrote a letter to the man releasing him from his offer, explaining the situation and that we may only get a few hundred pounds for our car.

The man once more said, "The price of my car is whatever money you get when you sell your car." God bless that family – they will never know just how much they helped us.

The Lord had done it again, and just before Christmas! We felt like it was a Christmas present directly from the Lord Himself. The kids loved it, especially its open-top roof. To be honest, when they were all getting a bit too noisy at times, we would allow them to go and play in the car – it was like another room for them. Our son Bobby's prayer had been answered in a most incredible way!

I hope this little story cheers you up in these lockdown days and encourages you to dare to pray big!

Stay safe and take care, love Diana

(Originally posted on 29th April 2020)

A Surprising Christmas

I remember a time just before Christmas, in the days when we **only** had three young children. We had no money yet again; in fact, we never seemed to have any money when the children were little. I didn't go out to work in those days. I had chosen for many reasons to stay at home until the children went to school. One of the main reasons was for the children to feel secure.

Anyway, we had no money for extras. We had just enough to get by and we didn't want to get into debt for Christmas like others may have done. I remember the Lord speaking into my heart, *Are you willing to do without earthly desires?*

I thought long and hard about the question and then agreed to it. Those earthly desires I felt were Christmas things, the whole materialistic side to Christmas. I had been thinking about and praying for many of the families surrounding our lives in those days.

These were the 'Thatcher days' when life was incredibly hard for people and the interest rates were up to 14 per cent! A lot of families were really struggling!

We received a cheque for £200, which was payment for a book that Mick had helped to write about debt. We had promised the Lord that if any money ever came from that book, then we would use it for the Lord's purposes, because the book had been written to help people.

There we were just before Christmas with the temptation of £200 to spend in whatever way we wished to. Mick and I spoke to the children and asked if they would be willing to forgo Christmas gifts that year and make our Christmas about giving? God bless them, as they all said, "Yes." I think that for children under the age of ten it was a big deal!

We decided to go and get all kinds of goodies to make up ten hampers, and then let the children come with us to deliver them. Together as a family, we all went to buy the 'goodies only' hampers, the sort of things that people who were struggling wouldn't have had the spare money to buy!

We made up the hampers into nice boxes and off we went to deliver them to the families in need who we knew were struggling. What joy and fun we had;

51

the kids loved it! I wish that you could have seen the joy on our kids' faces as we delivered those hampers; it really was the true joy of Christmas! I still felt a bit sad that we had no money to get our kids toys for Christmas, but God had a way of surprising us!

As we went to church on the Sunday before Christmas, no one knew that we hadn't a penny to spend to get our kids any Christmas presents! At church, a friend of mine gave me an envelope and said to me, "That is for your kids for Christmas." I looked inside the envelope and saw that it contained £100! I told my friend, "I can't take this." She assured me that the Lord had told her to give that amount.

On the way home from church, we went to Toys "R" Us and we got the kids toys that they had picked out, plus batteries, for just over £100. But God had not finished yet!

On the day before Christmas, I felt the Lord speak to me again, *What do you want, child?*

Lord, I would love some new clothes for everyone for Christmas.

I am not kidding you, but within an hour, someone had come and posted another £100 through our letter box. God had given back to our family what He had asked us to give away in the first place!

The Bible says, "It is more blessed to give than receive," and yes, we experienced the joy of that – it was pure joy! But God gave freely back to us and I personally felt like it was all just a test! By the way, the clothes that I managed to buy for everyone, I got for a third of the price that they should have been! My friends, you cannot out-give God, you just can't!

I hope this little story brings you joy in these challenging days. Stay safe and remember that God cares. He cared for us about stuff that wasn't so much a need but a desire. How much more will He care for you?

Stay safe and take care, love Diana

(Originally posted on 30th April 2020)

The Story of Lauren's Birth – Part One: The Day I Met the Lord

I remember when I was about to give birth to my daughter Lauren. I went to bed and was simply reading a book when my waters broke.

This was my third child, so I thought that we had better take the other two children to my in-law's house and then get me to the hospital. The hospital wanted me to go in because my waters had broken, but for some reason unknown to us at that time, the birth was not progressing as it should have been.

The hospital staff gave me some tablets which would usually bring the birth on. This was after I had stayed in hospital all night with nothing more happening. By lunchtime, the pains were getting stronger but there were still no signs of the baby coming. Since she was a third child, she should have been delivered quite quickly.

By mid-afternoon, my husband was telling the midwife that something must be wrong. He had seen me give birth twice before but this time it seemed different. The midwife began to get very concerned when I began to bleed heavily. A doctor was called to the delivery suite and he immediately sent for an ambulance to take me to another hospital. I knew something was very wrong because this was my third baby!

I was taken directly in an ambulance from Chorley Hospital to Sharoe Green Hospital in Preston. I didn't know the Lord in those days but I did believe in God and I knew how to pray – just like we all do in a crisis!

I prayed that the Lord would save this baby's life, not realising that my own life was also at risk. I told the Lord that, *I don't want to live without this baby, but my other children need me and so I need the baby to live.* I also said, *If you save this baby for me, I will dedicate my life to you!*

When we arrived at Sharoe Green Hospital, the delivery team quickly realised that a piece of afterbirth had come away during the pregnancy and it was blocking the birth canal. As the midwife catheterised me, she dislodged the blockage and the baby managed to be born.

There were so many doctors and nurses in the room by that point. There was a team working on my new-born baby girl Lauren and people working on me, trying to stop the bleeding. They told me that the operating theatres were just across the corridor and that I may have to be taken there if they couldn't stop the bleeding.

I prayed yet again and said to the Lord, *I have been through enough, please don't let me have to go to theatre.* The birth was an incredibly traumatic experience for me!

They finally placed my little baby girl in my arms after they had resuscitated her, and she looked beautiful! The midwife even said, "This is a bonny one."

They had to keep me in the delivery suite all night just in case I needed to go to theatre. By now, I was hooked up to a blood transfusion and they wanted to bring the baby back in to me, to put her to the breast, thinking that this might help the womb contract and stop the bleeding.

With one arm hooked up to the transfusion and my little baby girl at my breast in the other arm, I thanked God for the safe arrival of my little baby. *Thank you, God, for this little one!*

At that very moment, as I thanked God, the delivery suite was filled with the presence of the Lord! For me, it had been the most traumatic birth ever, but my baby girl was safe and so was I.

I never did have to go to the theatre and, a few days later, we were both well enough to go home. Then I went looking for answers about my God encounter, but that's tomorrow's story …

Stay safe and remember that you are loved and precious to God!

Love Diana

TO BE CONTINUED

(Originally posted on 1st May 2020)

The Story of Lauren's Birth – Part Two: The Encounter

I remember coming home with my new baby girl and being shocked and traumatised by her birth! I also started my search for God because of my encounter in the delivery suite.

I went to talk with the Catholic priest, knowing that something had happened in that room, but the priest was no help to me. I wanted to get Lauren christened asap because that was my way of getting God to protect her life, knowing that her birth had been her own fight for life as well as having been mine.

I think she was only about four weeks old when she was christened. I remember singing a song in a church service, knowing it was speaking to me but not really understanding what it was saying. The words of the song were:

> Here I am, Lord. Is it I, Lord? I have heard you calling in the night. I will go, Lord, if you lead me. I will hold Your people in my heart.

I was also talking to the Jehovah's Witnesses at that time in my search to get closer to God. One day, my Auntie Pauline, who was more of a friend than an auntie because there were only a few years' difference in our ages, came to my house and saw me talking with the Jehovah's Witnesses. As soon as they had left the house, Auntie Pauline said to me, "I believe you are searching for God. Read this booklet and let me know what you think!" It was a very small, thin

---

[22] Lauren aged just four weeks © Diana Wood, 1987

booklet called *Journey Into Life*, written by a man called Norman Warren. This book really changed my life, so it's no wonder it is called *Journey Into Life*!

Pauline returned and asked me what I thought about the book? I told her that it explained exactly what I was looking for, and it had made sense of my encounter in the hospital. There was a prayer at the back of the book that I prayed.

Pauline then took me to meet a man who would fully explain what had happened to me. His name was Pete Leigh, and he was a young local evangelist. When I got to Pete's house, there was a house group meeting going on and I began to feel a bit threatened. Anyway, I asked Pete if he would explain the Trinity to me and, if he could, I would become a Christian. Pete explained the Trinity to me in a way that I could understand, and then I went home to think about all that I had heard.

When I got home, I went to kneel at my bedside to talk with God. I told Him that I was sorry for all the things that I could think of that I had done wrong in my life. I then asked God to come into my life by His Holy Spirit.

Well, I cannot begin to tell you of the joy that filled my life at that moment! I went downstairs to where my husband was and I began to kiss his face all over with so many kisses. I think he must have thought that I had lost my mind. In reality, I had just fallen in love with Jesus.

Does anyone remember that feeling of first falling head over heels in love? That was me and so much more! I had never known the feeling of being fully loved before that point, even though I had a husband that I was besotted with. I had never known such a sense of joy and peace. All the emptiness that had filled my life, all my mistakes, had been put right, and I was loved by God so completely. I truly had journeyed into the fullness of life, and life would never be the same again!

As you have already seen from some of my stories, this is a relationship that will last for the rest of my life and on into eternity!

Stay safe and take care, love Diana

(Originally posted on 2nd May 2020)

Thankful!

There is much to thank God for!

- Years of holidays provided for, year after year, as the kids were growing up!
- Blessings out of nowhere that we didn't expect.
- Healings for family and friends, of which there have been many over the years, too many to mention!
- Uniform provided, and kids' shoes, too, as well as my own shoes at times.
- I have even found money in the street, with no one in sight to ask if it's theirs, when I have prayed for something I needed just before, e.g. shoes.
- Safe travel – even when we have been in accidents, God has kept us safe!
- Homes provided to live in, after praying.
- School places for the children's education.
- Cars when we have needed them.
- Clearing our debts in a single day, three years ago.
- Amazing people brought into our lives to share the journey with!
- The continuous supply of flour even in lockdown!
- Setting me free from all my fears, as I was such a fearful person.
- Jobs provided that have seemed tailor-made!
- My beautiful kids and the gift of grandchildren to love which, I believe, takes love to a whole new level!
- The biggest thank you is for the gift of my relationship with the Lord, which has been my constant source of love, security, counsel, and the deepest friendship imaginable!
- Thank you, Lord, for all these memories and so much more.

> Rejoice always, pray continually, give thanks in all circumstances; for this is God's will for you in Christ Jesus. **(1 Thessalonians 5:16–18)**
> **THANK YOU, LORD, FOR EVERYTHING!**

Stay safe and take care, love Diana

(Originally posted on 3rd May 2020)

The Summer of 1969

I was brought up on the Callen estate at the top end of New Hall Lane in Preston. I remember when a group of people began to build an adventure playground on the back fields where I lived.

It was a church group who built the playground for the kids from this poor estate to play on. They did a summer club in the holidays for around two weeks and we went to this club and the adventure playground. I remember watching them build it and being so excited that this was going to be on the edge of the fields at the back of our house where we played out daily.

During the summer of 1969, me and other kids from the estate joined the summer club for two weeks. The club was called "F.O.G.", which stood for "Friends of God".

When we had finished our two weeks at the club, we were invited to go to church. It was a little church called St Mary's and I think it was on St Mary's Street, just off New Hall Lane. They had a Sunday school at the church and I only went for around two Sundays. I distinctly remember staying behind on one of those Sundays and asking Jesus to come into my life.

After those two weeks, I never went again to St Mary's, but as I grew up, I was always aware that God was real. I prayed when I felt I needed to, especially when difficulties arose in my life.

I loved the assemblies at school and, looking back now, I can see that God was speaking to me through those assemblies. I just didn't fully realise or understand what He was saying at the time. I was so young and trying to make sense of it all wasn't easy.

When I was around nine years old, my new-born baby brother Jimmy was very ill. He had gone down in weight from 9lbs to 5.5lbs (4kg to 2.5kg). He was taken into hospital to try and find out what was wrong. He ended up having an operation because he had something wrong called a pyloric stenosis. (Pyloric stenosis is a problem that affects babies between birth and six months of age and causes forceful vomiting that can lead to dehydration.) My little brother was fighting for his life and I didn't know until we got a knock at our front door not long after going to bed.

It was a policeman, who had been sent by the hospital to get my mum to go to the hospital. I listened at the top of the stairs and I remember going back to my bedroom to pray. We lived in my grandad's house, so he was Mum's constant babysitter when needed.

I really prayed that night, as much as a small child knew how to pray! The doctors did manage to save my little brother by doing some experimental treatment that had never been done before. I think they put plasma in his brain! Now, was that God's answer to a little girl's prayer? I will never know this side of heaven, but I know this – my baby brother Jimmy survived the operation after being given the last rites by a priest, and came home to live with us again.

My mum always said that the plasma they put into his brain made him a bit loopy, and today he is one of the most witty and funny guys that I have ever met!

Thank you again, Lord, for prayers answered known and unknown. You truly are amazing! Stay safe, friends, and I hope you enjoyed this childhood memory.

Take care, love Diana

(Originally posted on 4th May 2020)

---

23 Jimmy © Jamieleigh Keaveney, 2018

Ordinary People, Extraordinary Miracles! – Part One

I remember when my little boy Bobby had eczema behind his ears. The eczema kept bleeding seemingly no matter what cream we used on it.

As a mum, I couldn't bear to see my son suffering. I decided to pray for healing for him every night when I took him to bed until this condition was healed. I decided that however long it took, I would pray until my prayers were answered. Within just two weeks, the eczema was gone, and it has never returned! Bobby is now thirty-five years old.

24

Our daughter Alexandra had a lot of work done on her teeth by the orthodontist. One of the things was that she was supposed to wear this very painful headgear to sleep in at nights and when she came home from school.

She would literally be in tears with the pain and I couldn't stand to see her suffering in that way. I decided to pray that the Lord would sort out her teeth

---

24 Bobby and Lauren © Mick Wood, 1994

supernaturally! I stopped her wearing the headgear after two weeks. I said no to any more of that pain for her, and that we just had to pray.

When we went back to the orthodontist some months later, I was expecting to be told off very severely for not making Alexandra persevere with the headgear. The orthodontist checked her teeth over and he said, "That seems to have done the job!" Alexandra looked at me, and me at her, with a silent knowing! The Lord had miraculously put those teeth where they needed to be. She never had to wear that painful headgear again!

My husband Mick had three growths on the outside of his neck. He had visited the hospital for a consultation and was waiting for a minor operation to have them all removed.

I sensed one day a strong urge to pray for those growths, so I spat on my fingers and placed them on the growths and prayed that God would get rid of them. I left it at that and never gave them another thought.

Mick got a letter from the hospital a few weeks later and we both realised that the growths had disappeared!

At what point they had disappeared we did not know – it could have been that very morning when I spat on them for all we knew – but they had all gone. God never ceases to amaze us, even today!

In case you are wondering, Jesus Himself healed a blind man using spit. In **John 9:1–7** we read of the following miracle:

> Now as Jesus was passing by, He saw a man blind from birth, and His disciples asked Him, "Rabbi, who sinned, this man or his parents, that he was born blind?"
>
> Jesus answered, "Neither this man nor his parents sinned, but this happened so that the works of God would be displayed in him. While it is daytime, we must do the works of Him who sent Me. Night is coming, when no one can work. While I am in the world, I am the light of the world."

When Jesus had said this, He spit on the ground, made some mud, and applied it to the man's eyes. Then He told him, "Go, wash in the Pool of Siloam" [which means "Sent"]. So the man went and washed and came back seeing.

I hope that these stories cause you to pray. You honestly never know what the Lord Jesus will do next, but this I know, He answers prayers!

Stay safe, love Diana

TO BE CONTINUED

(Originally posted on 5th May 2020)

Ordinary People, Extraordinary Miracles! – Part Two

I remember taking my children to school and the nursery school attached to it. I walked there with three children under five, one in the pram and two small children holding on to it. There was also another young mum with two children, one in a pram, and we walked home together with our prams and babies. This young woman became my lifelong friend and her family, too; her name is Karon.

Karon had just separated from her husband and she had to sell her little house and get a council house. I prayed for Karon and her little family that she would be able to get a house from the council. As I prayed, I really felt that the Lord had said that *Karon will have a house by the end of the month.*

I told her this and prayed that it would be so! As we were heading towards the end of the month, I prayed even more, as I didn't want my friend to be disappointed in God. It got to the 29th of the month and Karon phoned me, excitedly telling me, "Di, I've got a house! I hope it's got a phone point in so I don't have to pay for putting one in, and I hope it's got a garden," and so it went on.

I just said, "Karon, it will have everything that you need, because we have prayed for this house." When she went to view it that day, it had everything in it that she needed. It was a spacious, three-bedroom house with a phone point, and Karon still lives in it today with her daughter and grandchildren!

I saw God answer many prayers for Karon. One day, I walked up to visit her. We were going to do a Bible study together because Karon had just become a Christian. When I got there, Karon told me that she had forgotten that I was coming because she had felt very ill that day.

25

She felt like she was getting flu, and she had the most creasing headache. I said to Karon, "Do you believe that God heals, Karon?"

She looked at me and answered, "Not really."

"Do you believe that I believe God heals?"

She said, "Yes."

"Well, on that we will pray." I prayed for Karon and instantly she was healed! Karon broke into laughter at the surprise of it. Then she went to make us both a cuppa, laughing as she went; she was just astounded at what God had done for her.

I also remember one school holiday season. Our children and Karon and I had spent the whole week together having picnics in the park and going around to each other's houses. Karon was going on a well-earned break to Wales on her own with no kids. It was the Friday before Karon was to leave on the Saturday for Wales.

I had a really strong concern for Karon and the kids, so strong that at the end of the day, I ended up nipping around to Karon's house to pray for them all. After praying, I went home and said that "I'll see you when you get back."

---

[25] Karon and Laura in 2017. Laura has her own family now. © Laura Langton, 2020

On the Sunday, I got a call from Karon. "Di, Laura [Karon's daughter] is in hospital and she has meningitis." I was so shocked and went off to pray upstairs because of what I had just heard.

As I prayed, I felt the Lord say, *Laura is going to be all right!* I wanted to tell Karon but we didn't have mobile phones in those days.

I thought of ringing the hospital but I decided it wouldn't be right to do that. While I was doing all that thinking, Karon rang back. "Di, your kids will all have to take some antibiotic medicine because we have all been together last week. Someone will come round and drop it off to you."

I said, "I am so glad that you have rung back, as I wanted to tell you that Laura is going to be all right."

Karon said, "Yeah, yeah."

I think that she thought that I was just trying to reassure her, so I told her again, "Laura is going to be all right!" Laura did indeed fully recover with no side effects from the meningitis!

I didn't realise at that stage in my life what meningitis could do to a body. I know now and I know that God truly did a miracle for Laura. She has grown up into a lovely young woman with her own business and is currently studying at university for a degree as a mature student. She also has two little girls of her own now.

God is good, God is faithful, and God can be trusted!

Stay safe, precious friends, because God loves you and so do I.

Love Diana x

(Originally posted on 6th May 2020)

Escaped Unhurt!

I remember one Sunday we were on our way to church, travelling in the car with three children in the back. For some reason, Mick decided to take a short cut down a country lane. As we drove down the lane, we went around a hairpin bend and, as we did, we hit some black ice and the car went into a spin. As the car was spinning, another car was coming towards us. It looked like it was going to hit us head-on and I still remember seeing the horror on the face of the passenger in that car.

I honestly thought, *This is it; we are all going to Heaven.* I shouted out, "JESUS HELP US!"

Somehow, we managed to avoid hitting the car that was heading towards us, but our car kept spinning until we hit a ten-foot stone wall head-on. We managed to all get out of the car and got the children to safety on the side of the road. I was hugging them all and asking if they were OK. Surprisingly, everyone seemed OK. The police quickly arrived and an ambulance shortly thereafter. After we had been checked all over, we were taken home by the police. The car had to be towed away as it was a write-off. It was a company car and only three months old.

When we arrived back home, I immediately put my worship music on. I was disappointed that we hadn't got to go to church, but I was so thankful to God that my little family was safe and unharmed. As we praised God, and thanked Him for our safety, I remember seeing in my mind a picture of an angel with his back to the window screen of the car. His wings were covering the screen and reaching all around us.

I knew that God was showing me that He had protected us. Then my daughter Alexandra, who was around nine years old at the time, said to me, "Mummy, I have just had a picture. I saw a big angel with his back to the window and his arms around us in the car." Bless her, she was confirming my picture and she didn't know it. Well, I am telling you, we danced around our living room literally in thanks to God for protecting us and keeping us safe!

The following day, Mick went out with one of his work colleagues to see the car. Mick's colleague could not believe that I had walked away from the crash unhurt. The passenger side of the car was badly crushed, but I just know that God sent His angel to protect us as I had called on the name of Jesus to help us.

Whatever situation you may find yourself in, cry out to Jesus. He wants to help you, too!

We are not a particularly special family, but rather a family who have an incredible God. A God who delights to walk through all aspects of our lives alongside us. Thank you, Lord, once again for your goodness, mercy, and protection.

I called on the Lord in my distress and He answered me.
(Psalm 120:1a)

Stay safe, love Diana

(Originally posted on 7th May 2020)

Awakening From a Coma

I remember a day when my friend Carol and I had been to minister to a church in Blackburn. Carol had taken the word and I was leading the worship.

When I arrived home, my husband Mick told me that my mum had been on the phone to let me know that my brother was in hospital. He was very ill and in a coma. He had not displayed any vital life signs for the previous twenty-four hours.

Mick and I dashed down to the Royal Preston Hospital from Chorley as quickly as we could. I desperately wanted to support my mum in this situation.

When we arrived at the hospital, we saw that my brother had a ventilator breathing for him as he slept in a coma. I talked with my mum to assess the situation. She told me that the doctors had said to her that, "There have been no life signs for around twenty-four hours!"

She also told me that she had been talking to him and asked him to blink in response. She said that he was blinking in response to her questions. When

[6] Di with Alex in St Annes © Mick Wood, 2016

Mum told the nurses, I think they thought it was just an involuntary response and repeated back to my mum that there had been no signs of life for twenty-four hours.

I asked my mum whether she minded if I prayed for my brother. My family were not particularly open to me praying with them – or for them – in those days, but I didn't know what else to do in the situation.

Mum said, "Yes, it can't hurt to pray." I had been given the go-ahead, so I prayed. I cannot even remember what I prayed, but I then told my mum that, "I am going to go home to the kids."

As I prepared to leave the bedside, I saw some flashing lights over my brother's hospital bed; they were like long swords.

I told my mum that, "I think that angels are here." I decided to wait a little while longer and prayed silently. Then my brother began twitching and moving around like he was uncomfortable.

I began to speak out his name, "Alex," to awaken him. The next moment, he began to try and pull the ventilator out of his mouth. Mum and I then started shouting for the nurse and she came running to us.

The nurse helped Alex get the pipe out of his mouth and he was able to speak with us! Wow, I had been there to see my brother awake from a coma. I honestly believe that it was a direct answer to our prayers!

God was always astounding me in those days. We saw one miracle after another in answer to our prayers! If you need a miracle in your life, I implore you to pray. You just never know what God will do, even if the medical reports are negative.

Believe for the best and pray!

Stay safe, love Diana

(Originally posted on 8th May 2020)

A Call to Serve

I remember a time when I had only been a Christian for a couple of years. I was at my church one Sunday as normal when one of the elders there said these words to the congregation:

Will you be poured out like wine upon the alter for me,
will you be broken like bread to feed the hungry?

I was shaking from head to foot and I said yes to the Lord. To be honest, if God had asked me to die for Him at that point, I would have done so willingly, so strong was the call upon my life to serve God. I had no idea what God was asking me to do specifically, but that would be revealed in time.

Not long after this, I enrolled in a preaching course which lasted for ten months. The commitment was to attend one day a month with additional homework in between sessions. When I sensed God calling me to do that course, I was battling with Him. I was so incredibly shy and had zero self-confidence at all in those days. Anyway, after struggling with the idea, I finally said "Yes" and joined up for the course.

I remember going to speak at an old people's home and it was a disaster. I hadn't eaten all day and I dropped my notes all over the floor. I ended up reading my message but certainly not preaching it. I was so disappointed in myself! On the way home, I had to stop my friend from driving her car so that I could be sick, even though I hadn't even eaten anything that day. When I got back home, I said to the Lord, *I do not believe that you have called me to speak.* I thought to myself, *I will never be doing that again.* The Lord spoke to me and said:

Not by might nor by power, but by my Spirit, you will do it!
(Zechariah 4:6)

70

My friend Carol came round the next morning and told me what she felt the Lord was saying to her. She said that, one day, I would speak to large groups of people just like I would speak to people in my own front room.

That is exactly what God did. It wasn't an instant miracle or anything like that, but a continual stepping out in obedience when opportunities came. God, in time, caused me to be able to speak and be free from the fear of man and self-pride. This enabled me to conquer my shyness and drove away my worrying of what people would think of me.

God taught me along the way to give into His hands what little I had and that He would do something with it. Just like the story of the five loaves and two fishes in the Bible, a little boy gave his small lunch to Jesus and He blessed it, and it fed 5,000 people! (See **John 6:5–15**)

I didn't need to be self-sufficient, but to instead give what little I had into Jesus' hands, and with that I can do all things through Christ who gives me strength!

That's a part of my journey of how I began public speaking. Evolving from a petrified young woman to one who could do whatever God had asked of her! I hope that this encourages anyone who is being called to be bold and to step out for the Lord.

Stay safe, love Diana

(Originally posted on 10th May 2020)

A Call to Women's Ministry – Part One

I remember when my children were little and we went to Calvary Christian Fellowship (CCF), our church in Lostock Hall in Preston.

If you had children in Sunday school then you were expected to help out; even if you were not called to teach, you could be a helper in Sunday school. Two weeks out of six, I would help out in the Sunday school, looking after children in the eighteen months to three years age group, and I loved it.

I would sing to the little ones and tell them stories with a flannel board as they sat and had their drink and biscuits. In total, I worked in Sunday school for around six years. During that time, the lady in charge of the whole of the Sunday school approached me and asked me if I would be willing to take charge of running the whole of the Sunday school?

The Sunday school had many different age groups within it, and running it was a massive task. I told her that, "I will pray about it and get back to you."

---

[27] Children's dedication at Calvary Christian Fellowship, circa 1988. Pictured with the family are Pastor Rob Whittaker, Sunday School Leader Nadia Bowie and Elders John and Carmella Kay © Mick Wood, 1991

At that time, I was also involved with the CCF evangelism team, and doing lots of different outreaches with women. If I was to take on the responsibility of being the Sunday school leader, it would be a full-time job and I wouldn't be able to continue doing some of the other things that I was involved in. I prayed to see what the Lord would have me do.

As I prayed, I saw a picture of a fork in the road and I sensed the Lord saying, *You choose.* God was giving me the choice between children's and women's ministry. At that time, as I had three young children, I decided on the women's ministry because I already spent a lot of time with children and wanted some adult company. I know that this sounds like a selfish reason, but that was the choice I made. That was almost thirty years ago.

I have done women's work in many different formats over the years. From coffee mornings to meals out with the women, trying to develop friendships with them. I facilitated Bible studies and spoke at many different women's meetings in many different denominations of churches. I was in Women's Aglow and I held positions on the board.

I also ran a large meeting of women, where all of the women from churches across the Fylde coast got together. It was called "Women of Destiny".

I also had my very own women's ministry that God had given me. The vision I had was to develop "Precious Women", a women's ministry to show women how precious and valued they were to God. To turn the vision into reality, I developed a team and we delivered different conferences all over the North West.

It's amazing what we can do when God calls us to do it! Even as a mum of five children and living in a very busy household, there was still time to do so much to help and empower other women.

Tomorrow I will share about "Precious Women" and the vision that developed.

Stay safe, love Diana

TO BE CONTINUED

(Originally posted on 11th May 2020)

A Call to Women's Ministry – Part 2: The Birth of "Precious Women"

I remember when I had been organising women's meetings for the women of the Fylde coast under the banner of "Women of Destiny". One of the speakers that I had asked to come and talk was a woman called Jackie Bowler.

Jackie ran a church with her husband in Manchester and she also ministered in the prophetic and healing. Jackie asked me if I would help her to set up some women's meetings for her own worldwide group called "Winning Women".

Some of the churches from the Fylde coast began to hold their own "Winning Women" meetings. Jackie would also put conferences on where all of the groups would join together. I would go along to these conferences as a supporter of "Winning Women".

When I was taking part in all of these different meetings, people would get confused, wondering and asking, "Is this Women of Destiny or Winning Women?" I began to seek the Lord as to which one I should be doing, because people were getting confused.

I remember going to a conference with Carol Halton, my very dear friend and prayer partner for many years. Carol and I were talking about whether to set up a women's ministry that was different and unique from what we were already doing. We were talking and praying in the car as we travelled. We arrived at the conference and enjoyed the day.

As the meeting was coming to a close, Jackie said, "I have a few words to give out to three different people" and one of those words was for me. I had always been a 'jack of all trades, master of none', or so I thought, but then Jackie spoke directly to me.

"Diana, you have your finger in many pies, but the strong call upon your life is for women!"

Carol and I thought that was a direct answer to our prayers. Jackie had no idea about our conversation in the car on the way over to the conference.

Carol and I began to seek the Lord for a clear vision of what God wanted us to do. God showed me through different scriptures that this new women's ministry would be built on the word of God and life experience. This new ministry would be called "Precious Women" because women were of high value and great worth to God!

The vision was to 'Empower, Encourage, and Equip' women to lead fuller lives. We designed days that any woman could come to and feel comfortable at, whether they were a Christian or not. God loved them and wanted them to live life in the fullness that He had created them for!

We produced teachings on overcoming fears and living confidently, building better relationships, love, and marriage, and looking good and feeling great, which included a whole section on dealing with stress. The Lord showed me that it was to be like medicine. You had to make it taste good and look good for people to swallow it. It was to be like a box of chocolates, designed in such a way that people would eat the word of God that was good for them, rather than spitting it out!

I loved this ministry that God had helped me to design and develop. It was unique and different to anything else that was going on at that time. I loved helping the women. I also loved seeing lives change through these day conferences. What a joy to do that kind of work!

Whatever God gives you to do, do it with all that is in you, and there will be great rewards for it.

Carol walked this path with me for a while, but God brought another along the road to help me called Lucinda Irvine, a beautiful woman of God that I met on my mission trip to Russia.

Stay safe, love Diana

TO BE CONTINUED

(Originally posted on 12th May 2020)

28

---

[28] Lucinda Irvine – Pskov, Russia, 2002 © Mick Wood, 2002

A Call to Women's Ministry – Part 3: Moving Forward

I remember sometime after starting "Precious Women" with Carol that Carol was offered a position with "Winning Women" to work with overseas missions. This was Carol's heart and she felt that it was time to move on with the mission side of things and to step away from "Precious Women".

I was left wondering what to do, as I didn't feel that I could run that ministry on my own, even though God had given me a very clear vision for it. I didn't see myself as a leader. Personally, I have always felt happier in a supporting role rather than the one leading.

Carol said to me, "Put it to bed and pray about it." That's exactly what I did for eighteen months, continuing to pray about it.

During this time of praying and seeking God for direction, I went over to Northern Ireland to visit my friend Lucinda Irvine, who I had met on my mission trip to Russia. Lucinda was helping host a Joyce Meyer conference the following weekend. Lucinda had invited me and another friend from the Russia mission trip to come and spend time at her house and go to the conference whilst we were over there.

It was very exciting spending time behind the scenes with Lucinda, who was doing many practical things to prepare for the conference, and we were able to help in very small ways.
The conference was wonderful, but the Lord still had not spoken to me about "Precious".

A few days after the conference was over, Lucinda and I, plus the other friend, were having a prayer time in Lucinda's lounge. Lucinda had no idea that I had been seeking the Lord about "Precious", but she spoke a scripture to me that hit my heart like a sledgehammer:

---

*Don't be afraid, for I am with you. Don't be discouraged, for I am your God. I will strengthen you and help you. I will hold you up with my victorious right hand. (**Isaiah 41:10**)*

This is how I heard and interpreted that word to me. I felt that God was very loudly saying to me, *Don't look around for who is going to help you, I myself will help you with this ministry!* I was astounded – if Almighty God was going to help me, then I could do this!

The funny thing, though, is that it was Lucinda who had spoken those very words to me from the Lord, and she was the one who came to help me. I made her a director of "Precious" and we worked together for many years, taking our day conferences to the North West of England.

My friends, if God calls you to do something, He will help you to accomplish it, even if you feel unqualified. Rick Yancey once said, "God doesn't call the equipped, but He equips the called."

Now all glory to God, who is able through His mighty power at work within us, to accomplish infinitely more than we might ask or think.
(Ephesians 3:20)

Stay safe, love Diana

* My Sister Deborah's Birthday

Today we would have celebrated your birthday with you, Deb – you would have been sixty. But today, I thank God for our wonderful memories, of a life filled with love for one another, loved and cherished in my heart forever, dear beautiful sis xxx

[29]

(Originally posted on 13th May 2020)

---

[29] Mt sister Debbie - © Amy King, 2020

A Brand-New House

I remember when we had been living in St Annes for seven years. Mick and I had just returned home from a two-week cruise in the Mediterranean. We began to open the post upon arriving home and in that batch of post was a notice to quit the house that we were living in. We had to be out of the house in twelve weeks' time. That meant that we would have to find a new home and be moved into it by the time that twelve weeks was up.

We still had four kids living at home with us, so this would not be an easy task on what we could afford. Anyway, we went to view quite a few houses, but none seemed in really good condition. They would need a lot of repairs, decorating, etc., and I didn't really want to have to start doing up another house at that point.

I saw this beautiful house at the top of the rentals list, which also meant that it was the highest price, certainly beyond what we could afford. I remember thinking, *Wouldn't it be good if we could go up to that price, because that house would be perfect for us to live in!*

Then I just dismissed it from my mind. Mick and I were viewing a house near to where we lived but it was not suitable; it needed so much doing to it. We told the estate agent that we were ideally looking for something that didn't need decorating.

He told us, "There is a house that I could show you, but it is beyond your budget. But I think that the owner may be willing to come down to the top of your budget."

So, we said, "OK, we will view the house seeing as you think that the owner may come down in price to what we can afford."

Apparently, the house had been up for sale for a year and hadn't sold. The owner had decided that he wanted to rent it for a few years rather than have it empty. We needed a long-term rental, so it would potentially suit both the owner and us very well.

The house was next door to a funeral parlour. That's the reason I think it wasn't selling, although at least the neighbours were quiet. The house had been totally renovated and decorated by a 'proper' designer. It had a brand-new kitchen with two ovens; four bedrooms; and three bathrooms, with a downstairs loo; plus, a massive lounge and dining area, with French doors across the wall at the back. The house was filled with light; even the hall and stairs had the most beautiful long window, which was on the landing halfway up the stairs. The house even had designer curtains in it to match the decor perfectly. I felt like I was a new bride starting life in a dream home!

The estate agent rang the owner, who said that he was willing to drop the price of the rent by £200 a month! This made the cost of the rent exactly the same as our maximum budget.

On the way out of the house, we noticed that the gatepost had something written on it, but it was faded. As we looked closely, we could see that the house was called 'Woodville'. As our surname is Wood, we felt that it was a sign from heaven.

30

We moved in and the owner never once increased the rent. Many people came to stay with us for holidays, and we even had four people come and stay who were on a mission in Blackpool.

---

[0] Woodville, Ansdell, Lytham St Annes © Mick Wood, 2020

We were able to host many events at that house. It was perfect for entertaining and catering for large groups of people. A God-given, perfectly designed house for our needs at that time in our lives.

We lived in that house for ten years, until our last grown-up daughter had left home. Mick and I moved on from that home to a ground floor apartment near the front at St Annes.

We still live there now and are very happy there, just two minutes from the beach. God knows our every need and is well able to supply them.

---

*My God will supply all my needs according to His riches in glory. **(Philippians 4:19)***

Stay safe, love Diana

(Originally posted on 14th May 2020)

A Call Up Higher

I remember a time when I was leading the worship group at the church I was attending at that time. I would travel across to "Abundant Life Church" in Bradford once every two months. They would put on days training for anyone in leadership of any kind within Church life. These training days were called "Build the House".

On one particular Saturday, I felt that the Lord was clarifying a call to deeper service for me. Previous to this, I had sensed God calling me to a particular role of service for Him as I daily read my bible.

I also heard the Lord speak to me as I visited a local church one Sunday evening. He was speaking to me as I sang a worship song called "The Potter's Hand" by Hillsong Worship. Through the words of the song, I sensed the Lord speaking to me. This is what I heard:

I am calling you up higher, I am calling you to something that you will be anointed in public to do!

I was left wondering, *How will this come about, because the church that I am attending at this point in time doesn't really do that kind of thing?*

I was still not sure of exactly what God was calling me to. Sometimes, when God speaks to us, it can be like giving you a jigsaw piece, a piece that you don't quite know how is going to fit into the puzzle. The day of real clarity came at "Build the House" in Bradford.

Paul Scanlon was speaking when God brought the clarity. This is what was said: "What is God calling you to do? Name it, define it, and God will empower it!" All of a sudden, I knew clearly what God had been trying to tell me over many months:

Name it? Deacon.

Define it? One who serves the Church.

God is going to empower me when I am anointed in public to do it!

Then I thought, *How am I going to tell our church leadership this? They will think that I am very brazen, to say the least*, but I didn't need to worry, because God had already gone before me.

The very next day, just before church began, the overseeing Pastor John Schofield said to me, "Congratulations, by the way." I asked John what he meant but he walked away as he was busy. *That was strange*, I thought.

After the service, John and two of the church leaders approached me. "We would like you to come on to the leadership team. We have been praying about it and feel that we should ask you. Will you pray about it?"

I told them that I didn't need to pray about it because God had already been speaking to me. Then I told them what the Lord had been saying to me about being a deacon. I didn't mention the public-anointing bit. If that was going to happen, I wanted God to bring that about, not me.

Two weeks later, Pastor John Schofield was anointing me with oil, to serve the Lord as a deacon, as someone who serves the Church. As John prayed for me, I felt like I had been living for this moment my whole life. I sensed a Holy Mantle being placed upon my shoulders. This was not an earthly thing but a call of God.

My lovely dad was sat in the congregation that Sunday, too, and it all just felt so right. Today is the day of my dad's funeral and I wanted to tell a story that he was a part of.

Stay safe and love your family today; they are God's precious gift to us!

God bless you all, love Diana

31

(Originally posted on 15th May 2020)

---

31 My dad, Alexander Brian Singleton © Diana Wood, 2015

First Love

I remember back when I had not long asked Jesus into my life. I honestly felt that I had fallen head over heels in love. I don't know if you remember how it felt to be walking down the road to meet the love of your life, with so much love and joy in your heart that you wanted to skip down the road, rather than walk?

That's how I felt when I first fell in love with Jesus. The love that the world had denied me, or had always come up short with, I now had in absolute abundance! In the mornings, I couldn't wait to get back from dropping the children off at school so that I could just sit in His presence and talk to Him; to drink in the wonder of Him!

When I first fell in love with Mick, if he was in the house, I just wanted to be in the same room that he was in. If he went for a bath, I would be washing his hair or scrubbing his back. Nothing was too much trouble because love wants to express itself.

32

"Love must find expression, or it is not love" (paraphrased from a quote by R. Mildred Barker). To me, that's saying love is an action word, a doing word.

One of the names of Jesus is "Wonderful Counsellor" and for quite a number of years Jesus was unravelling the mess of my life; helping me make sense of things and deal with them. He gave me back confidence that life's hurts had taken away from me. He would give me insight into how He saw me.

---

32 Me and Mick © Alexandra Hodgson, 2015

Have you ever looked at yourself through the eyes of love? You begin to see yourself in a better way, rather than feeling rubbish about yourself because that's how you had always been treated previously, as rubbish.

I would sometimes be doing my housework, and I would sense Jesus saying to me, *Leave that and come and talk to me.* I remember once walking around town worrying about something, and then thinking to myself, *What are you doing? Go home and pray about it.*

In these lockdown days, I feel that I have been robbed of relationships. Robbed of not being able to spend time with my grandchildren. Robbed of not being able to show love by hugging them, that's if I get to see them at all. Robbed of spending time with friends, of socialising, swimming, and days out, robbed of so many things that would lift my spirit.

Today, I was robbed at my dad's funeral, where I couldn't even hug my kids or family at such a sad time. I am sick of waiting for lockdown to be over.

I have decided that I am just going to use this time to go deeper with Jesus. Return to that deep first love, of just loving to be with Him. Returning to the wonder of just knowing Him and loving Him. I will be fruitful in my isolation! And what the enemy intended to rob me of, I will have more with Jesus than this world could ever give me!

Yes, I will still enjoy my beautiful, God-given family on FaceTime or sitting isolated at a distance in a cold back garden, as I wait patiently to demonstrate my love by putting my arms around those whom God has given me to love. Until then, I can show them through my words, help them where I can, send little gifts of love, like baking for the grandchildren or making Nana's hotpot that they love so much. And maybe, just maybe, my time spent closer to Jesus will somehow bless their life, too, as I pray for them all.

In these lockdown days, try and use this time for a better life in the future, or a better life right now. Do what you can to stay positive and feel a sense of purpose. May I suggest that if you need to feel love in this world, get to know Jesus. You will not be disappointed. That I can totally guarantee!

We love because he first loved us. Whoever claims to love God yet hates a brother or sister is a liar. For whoever does not love their brother and sister, whom they have seen, cannot love God, whom they have not seen. And he has given us this command: Anyone who loves God must also love their brother and sister. **(1 John 4:19–21)**

God bless you all, love Diana

(Originally posted on 16th May 2020)

Mick Becomes a Christian

I remember when I first became a Christian, Mick wouldn't allow me to take the children to church, only the new baby (Lauren). He was a Catholic and he didn't want the children 'influenced', so I respected that and took my new baby off to church on a Sunday morning on the bus.

Mick would pick me up from church so that I could get home to make the Sunday lunch. He was supportive when I got baptized, but I wasn't allowed to play my Christian music in the house if he was in. He was very anti-Christian really and not easy to live with because of the differences in our faith. We lived like that for the first two years of my Christian faith walk.

One very sad day, Mick's friend was killed instantly on his way to work; a lorry had jack-knifed in front of his car and Mick's friend had been killed instantly. This man had been like a fatherly mentor to Mick and his death badly affected Mick. I was praying about it all and felt that somehow God would use this sorrow to bring Mick to really know God personally.

Two weeks after Mick's friend Jack had died, I was praying to the Lord about Mick coming to church with me. There was a special service on for people that didn't really know Jesus. I decided that I would not ask Mick to come with me, because it had to come from him. I went downstairs and Mick said to me, "I think that I will come with you this morning."

Wow! This was the man who was constantly anti-Christian. I was overjoyed but tried to play it cool and just said, "OK."

Mick came to church that Sunday and I had to hold Lauren in my arms to shield him from seeing me crying. My emotions had been stirred up by all that was happening.

That morning, there was a guy telling his life story. Mick felt like the guy could have been speaking to just him. It was so relevant for Mick. We went home in the car and I hardly dared ask him about it in case he got angry about it. When I finally got the courage up, I asked him, "How did you feel about the service?" I could tell that God had spoken to Mick that morning.

I was going back to church that evening, so I left Mick with a book to read called *Journey into Life*. I told him that we would talk about it when I returned home from church that evening.

On returning home, I discovered that Mick had asked Jesus to come into his life, to forgive him of all the wrong things that he had done. Also, that he wanted to follow Jesus for the rest of his life.

That decision cost Mick and our children dearly. It brought about a split with Mick's mum, who was an Irish Catholic. She thought that Mick had betrayed his heritage and she disowned him. After being in Northern Ireland many times, I could understand her thinking. Many lives had been lost over religion. Bless her, she didn't understand that Mick had a newfound faith in God rather than a religious way of living. As a committed Christian, Mick could go to any church of his choice, but he wanted to go to a church that was more relevant for him rather than just follow a set of religious rules.

Within four years of Mick becoming a Christian, he had set up a Christian charity called "The Harvesters Trust". The charity went on to give money to people and organisations in more than forty countries around the world. The charity funded a school in Argentina, an orphanage in Zambia, put wells in villages in Africa, provided Christian Literature for Ugandan schoolchildren, and funded feeding programmes in Russia and Argentina, just to name a few of those works. He has helped write two books on debt for the Evangelical Alliance and achieved many more amazing things as he lives out his life with Jesus by his side.

With God, all things are possible; keep the faith, keep praying, keep believing.

Religion that God our father accepts as pure and faultless is this. To look after orphans and widows in their distress and to keep oneself from being polluted by the world. **(James 1:27)**

God bless you all, love Diana

(Originally posted on 18th May 2020)

---

[33] One project involved sending a truckload of Christian books over to Uganda © Mick Wood, 2010

Daily Interruptions

I remember when life was so busy – bringing young children up, trying to keep the home running smoothly – it seemed such a mammoth task.

I would arrive back home after dropping the children off at school, after what seemed like 'stress intensified'. I would ignore the housework that was beckoning me and leave it all to sit and read my bible and pray. Time to regain my sanity. The washing seemed unending, especially with three children.

When we went from three to five children, I would feel like a hamster on a wheel, going nowhere, only round and round. I was constantly playing catch-up, but I needed an orderly house for my own mental health and wellbeing.

Even when life was so busy with all those things, my house was like a drop-in centre. I lived in a terraced house in Chorley town centre, near to one of the main shopping streets. It was ideal for people to drop in for a coffee whilst they were out shopping.

People would come to chat about their problems, have a cuppa, and I would pray for them before they left the house. We were constantly running out of tea and coffee, milk and sugar. Sometimes, I would think to myself that I needed to get on with the housework before the kids and hubby got home.

I remember reading something one morning that completely changed my thinking on the interruptions. It was probably one of my daily reading books that went with a Bible reading. I remember it said, "Lord will you please stop the interruptions, so that I can get on with my work." Then I felt the Lord say …

---

*The interruptions **are** the work!*

I hadn't realised that what I was doing was providing a service to God's people, the people that He loved so very much. After this revelation, I never struggled with that kind of thinking again.

Many times, I would be at my door waving someone off and I could see the next person coming up the street to visit me. I learnt to do the housework in the evening when the kids had gone to bed, thus freeing up my days for people.

People have always been the most precious gift in my life. I love people, I love listening to them, to understand what makes them tick. I even went to college as a mature student at the age of thirty-four, to study Psychology and Sociology, and people still fascinate me.

I don't have hobbies, but I seem to collect people. We even added some to our family as extended family members. My kids also love people, because our house has always been full of them over the years. In these lockdown days, it has been difficult not to be with people, but I ring them or write to them instead. God made us for relationship, with Him and each other.

Love the Lord thy God with all your heart, mind and strength and love your Neighbour as yourself. **(Matthew 22:37)**

The two most important commandments according to Jesus. Maybe after lockdown, we will all value each other just that little bit more than we did before.

God bless, strengthen, and help you in these very trying days.

Love Diana

(Originally posted on 19th May 2020)

Big Changes, Including Attitude

I remember when we had just taken two more children into our home. Very sadly, their mum had died with cancer aged twenty-eight. My brother was the father of the children, but he had never lived with Donna, the children's mum.

My mum had always given Donna support over the years and even nursed Donna as she died at home. Donna's death affected us all in different ways. To see someone suffer with cancer at such a young age left its mark on us all.

I was still grieving when we took on these two young children. I was struggling emotionally and physically. Many times, as I took the children up to bed at night, my legs would feel like lead. I was totally exhausted.

34

As I prayed with the children and sang over them before they went to sleep, I could feel the Holy Spirit fall upon me to strengthen me.

There were many lessons I learnt in those early days of having five kids instead of three. One of the biggest lessons was that, if I kept a good attitude, I had

---

34 Jennifer and Jacob © Mick Wood, 1995

what I needed energy wise to do the job. If I started feeling resentful about my workload, then I would lose my energy and things seemed ten times worse.

I must stress here, it was the workload that came from having extra children, not from loving two extra children, who as kids were always a joy to me.

The Bible says in **Proverbs 4:23**, "Guard your heart, for from it flow the well springs of life."

I have learnt over the years that my heart has needed guarding: guarding against resentment, guarding against bitterness, guarding against jealousy of others, guarding against anger. All these bad emotions literally drain one's energy and strength. By contrast, the Bible says, "The joy of the Lord is my strength." **(Nehemiah 8:10)**

The joy of the Lord is more evident in my life when I keep my heart right. When I start having issues with people, and a bad heart attitude, then that strength quickly evaporates.

Even now, many years down the road, I am still guarding my heart from the lesson I learned in those early days.

Whatever life brings our way, sometimes circumstances can be difficult to live with. Sometimes we cannot change our circumstances, but we can always change our attitude. It also starts by accepting that, "This is where I am at right now. I cannot change what has happened in my life, but I can change how I am going to cope with it."

Good attitude that brings me joy and strength, or bad attitude that drains me and makes me miserable and joyless. The choice is mine.

We are all living in unprecedented times, and we may not be able to change that. We can, however, change our attitude in how we make our way through these times.

Stay safe, dear ones, you are very loved by God.

Love Diana

(Originally posted on 20th May 2020)

Flooded With Peace in a Time of Distress

I remember a time in 1995. Every weekend, we had been having the two children stay with us, the two children that would shortly be added to our family, so that they could get accustomed to us as a family. We were preparing for the death of their mother Donna whilst all the time still hoping for a miracle for her.

The children came to stay with us one weekend; it was three weeks before Donna died. That weekend, Donna became very ill, and the children never went home again. Donna even said goodbye to her little girl over the phone, telling her that the angels were there with her; very, very sad days!

35

My mum was helping nurse Donna at home with the Macmillan nurses. On the Thursday morning, just before Donna died in the early hours of the Saturday morning, I rang my mum to ask how Donna was. This was something I had done every day for the previous few weeks. This particular day when I asked how Donna was, my mum replied, "She's decaying."

---

35 Donna with Jennifer and Jacob in 1994 – one year before she died © Mick Wood, 1994

"What do you mean, 'She's decaying'?"

My mum went on to say, "Her ear is like a bad apple going black, her legs are, too, and cancers are popping out of her head."

I was absolutely distraught when I came off the phone and began to cry. I was even angry at God, asking Him, *How can you let this happen? Why have you not taken her to be with you before now? She belongs to you.*

God instantly gave me an answer to that question. He gave me the following verses from **2 Corinthians 4:16–18**. This is how I remember the verses now:

Though outward we are decaying, yet inward we are being renewed day by day and our light and momentary troubles are preparing for us an eternal glory that will far outweigh it all.

I felt that God was saying to me, *I am doing a work in Donna that you know nothing about. What I have for her in eternity will make up for all this suffering!*

Instantly, peace flooded my soul and I stopped crying.

God's ways are not our ways. Sometimes, we really feel distressed at what we see with our eyes, but do you know …

"Even when we don't see it, He is working. Even when we don't feel it, He is working. He never stops, never stops working."

These are words from a song called "Way Maker" by SINACH and they are very true.

You may have questions in these difficult days. God may answer them, or He may say, *Not yet*. No matter what, you can be assured He will be working in it all.

God bless you all and keep you safe.

Love Diana

(Originally posted on 21st May 2020)

---

36 Donna, August 1995 © Mick Wood, 1995

Loving Difficult People

I remember a time, when I was sixteen years old, that I worked in a café in Preston on Fishergate called the Monte Carlo Coffee Bar. I loved it there. We had a little elderly lady who worked with us there who washed the dishes. Her name was Dorothy.

37

Bless her, she would have to carry them up and down from the basement, and I thought that the boss was unkind to her. I would deliberately be nice to her, to try and make up for his harshness. We formed a friendship that was to last thirty years. Even when we moved to St Annes, she would come to visit me.

Most Fridays, for years, I styled her hair, setting it or perming it, and would then make her a nice lunch. When the children came along, I found it difficult, but still continued the routine. The longer that time went on, the ruder and more difficult she became. She lost her husband and I honestly think that she was getting some kind of dementia. In those days, we were not so informed about it as we are today. I cared about her but she was not easy to be with. When the children were little, she would hit them on the head for no reason. Looking back, they were probably an annoyance to her.

She wanted my time and undivided attention, which I couldn't totally give because of the children. She did some really bizarre things and would absolutely talk my ears off. I remember saying to her one day, "Dorothy, if you hit my kids, you won't be able to come again!" She used to say all sorts of unkind

---

[37] Dorothy © Diana Wood, 1998

things to me, but I excused it because of her age. Sometimes, I would challenge her behaviour whilst trying not to be rude in return.

I remember one day going into the kitchen, keeping out of her way, and saying to the Lord, *She's driving me mad, why do you keep sending her here to me?* The Lord said in reply, *I am teaching you to love the unlovely.*

One day, Dorothy was talking to me about heaven because of the loss of her husband. I ended up telling Dorothy how to become a real Christian. Dorothy had gone to church most of her life but she didn't really know the Lord. She asked Jesus to come into her life and she changed. She taught herself to play the keyboard and sang hymns most mornings. We no longer had to put up with her strange behaviour.

I remember going across to Chorley Hospital to visit her as she was dying and in a coma. As I prayed with her, no one else was there. Then my eldest daughter Alexandra arrived and I told Dorothy that Alexandra was there, and a tear ran down her face. Even though she was supposed to be in a coma, her hand gripped mine as I prayed for her before I left her side.

I literally had to take her fingers off my hand one by one as I said my last goodbye. I prayed with her and told her that I would see her again in heaven. I felt privileged that I could be a part of ushering her out of this world. There was no denying the love that was in that room that day. The woman who had literally driven me to distraction at times was loved so completely.

God teaches us some difficult life lessons at times, but the benefits far outweigh the difficulties.

Love never gives up, never loses faith, is always hopeful and endures through every circumstance. **(1 Corinthians 13:7)**

The greatest gift we can have on this Earth is to love and be loved in return.

Stay safe in these days and show love to others in any way that you can. You will always have the benefit of it. Love and blessings to you all, Diana

(Originally posted on 27th May 2020)

The Glory Wagon

I remember a time when we had no car. The car that we'd had previously was linked in with a job that Mick had, but his job had come to an end through no fault of his own.

Some good friends of ours worked in a deprived area of Preston, where we had been helping them build a church on the estate. We taught very practical teachings for the people of the estate. For example, dealing with disciplining children, with stress, with finances and debt, with marriage, and many other topics. We really loved those people and we saw over thirty from the estate come to faith in Jesus in less than a year during our time working with them.

We were overwhelmed one day when some of this group from Preston arrived at our house in Chorley. They had found out via the church leaders, Dot and Kev, that Mick was without a job and that we were struggling financially. They had realised that we couldn't get to their estate because we had no car.

Anyway, this group from the estate turned up, bringing with them food and money that they had collected for us. They arrived in a big blue makeshift minibus that we fondly named the "Glory Wagon". We were very humbled by such overwhelming generosity from these financially very poor people. The joy that was on their faces from coming and doing that gesture for us was a gift in itself.

We have never forgotten such overwhelming kindness in our time of need.

Dot and Kev also lent us the Glory Wagon for a while, until we got a car of our own. The kids hated it because they had always been used to having new company cars over the years. It was a lesson in humility for us all, but we grew to love the Glory Wagon, because it had been lent to us with such love and genuine care.

The Glory Wagon even took us all the way to Skegness, to "Spring Harvest", which was a Christian conference for families that was held at the Butlins site there. It was ideal for young families to have all the pleasure of the pool and fairground, as well as all the kids' activities and clubs of the conference. We got to go for free because Mick was working voluntarily as a debt counsellor at that time with an organisation called "Credit Action".

We had a fabulous time as a family, even with Mick working. What an adventure that was. We had to get help to start the van up again after two weeks

99

of being there because it had a flat battery, but it got us home safely, the wonderful Glory Wagon.

God has taken care of us in so many situations over the years, faithfully, kindly, generously, and humbly at times. He knows exactly what we need in every situation, even if it humbles us.

God is changing our character each day if we allow Him, and it's always for our good.

The following Bible verses remind me of the people on the estate at Preston:

Now I want you to know, dear brothers and sisters, what God in His kindness has done through the churches in Macedonia. They are being tested by many troubles, and they are very poor. But they are also filled with abundant joy, which has overflowed in rich generosity. For I can testify that they gave not only what they could afford, but far more. And they did it out of their own free will. They begged us again for the privilege of sharing in the gift for the believers in Jerusalem. They even did more than we had hoped, for their action was to give themselves to the Lord and to us, just as God wanted them to do. **(2 Corinthians 8:1–5)**

Be encouraged by these people's generosity as I am also being personally challenged in these lockdown days. Who can I give to?

---

[38] Mick at Credit Action © Mick Wood, 1992

Stay safe. We are not through this yet, so keep pressing on one day at a time. Remember that today has enough troubles of its own, but we **will** get through this!

God bless you all, love Diana

(Originally posted on 29th May 2020)

The Gift of True Friendship

I cannot finish this book without sharing a very important part of my life. This story did not go on Facebook, but my book would not be complete without it. It is a story of God's love and faithfulness to me.

I am blessed to have many God-given, trusted friends who live all over the world. I see all of them as special gifts from my heavenly Father to me. They mean the world to me and I could write a story for each one of them, and of their love and goodness towards me over the years. I always thank God for the gift of them, but this story is about two particular friends.

I remember back in 1999, I met a couple who came along to our church one particular Sunday. They were brought to the church by mutual friends who were part of the leadership team of our church at that time. As I looked at the woman's face, I could see that she was filled with anxiety. I remember thinking to myself, *You are where I have just been.*

I had just come through a difficult period in my life, when I had felt like I was on the edge of a breakdown. I suffered from anxiety and panic attacks, and I could literally see those same things in this woman's face. I invited this new couple to come to my house for lunch. Considering her issues at that time, it was amazing that the woman came at all.

We soon became great friends; we just hit it off immediately. As we chatted, we realised that our paths had crossed many times before. One of those times had been when Max (the husband) had become a Christian. I was helping in a café that evening at Chorley Elim Church. A mutual friend, Debbie, came and asked me and another lady if we would pray for this woman. Her husband had just gone upstairs to give his life to Jesus and had gone to speak with the pastor of that church. We had also seen them a few other times before we became really good friends. Max and Stella very quickly became like family to us.

They regularly came across to St Annes to have Sunday roast with us. Afterwards, we would walk up to a beautiful, relaxing bar and just sit there having lovely coffees. The bar was called Joya and we often would go for a light lunch or afternoon tea with our newfound friends.

Stella came to stay with me when Mick went to work in California for a couple of weeks. Max wanted to get some decorating done and this would cause anxiety for Stella, so it suited us both for Stella to come and stay with our family. She loved it and would even get up early to see the kids off to school with me.

Stella was the very first visitor to stay with us at our home in St Annes; there would be many others over time. We laughed so much when she stayed; in fact, we laughed every time we met for the next twenty years!

Stella was a very insightful, sensitive, and empathic woman. She was a great encourager in all that I did. She prayed for me whenever I was going to speak somewhere; in fact, she would always be covering me with her prayers. She was a great listener and brilliant counsellor. She would tell you the truth even if you didn't like what she said. It was given with such love that one could never be offended.

The Bible says, "An honest answer is like a kiss on the lips." **(Proverbs 24:26)** Stella had the ability to see things in my heart that only God knew about me; she 'got' me and likewise I understood Stella, too.

For many years, they lent us their lovely caravan in Wales to have holidays with our kids. They would come week after week with treats for the kids, and for Mick and me as well. They helped us in more ways than I could ever count.

39

---

³⁹ Max, Stella Di and Mick in 2008 © Mick Wood, 2008

Max is also one of the most generous, wisest, and understanding people that we have ever had the privilege to meet. A man full of integrity, as was Stella, too, and anyone who met them would say the same. These friends were God-given into our lives.

Their goodness towards us surrounds our lives in many ways; our home is full of gifts given by them over the years. We have albums full of photographs of special days filled with happy memories.

The Bible says, "There is a friend that sticks closer than a brother" **(Proverbs 18:24)** and "A brother is born for adversity" **(Proverbs 17:17)**. When life threw adversity at us, these dear friends stayed, listened, helped where they could, and stuck close like the good brother and sister that they were. In some ways, they have been better than family.

We went on holidays together, shared Christmas, Easter, anniversaries, and birthday celebrations. We even had two weeks together on a Mediterranean cruise for our twenty-fifth wedding anniversary and Stella and Max's fortieth anniversary. Max even had his seventieth birthday celebration in our home. We made him a boxing ring cake with two boxing gloves on top. Max loves watching the boxing.

Stella died in 2018 on Boxing Day, very suddenly and unexpected. Our whole family were shaken to the core. It was like a bomb had gone off and left this big hole in our lives. My dearest sis, who I talked to every day, had gone from my life and the life of our family.

Max still comes to see us and shares in family celebrations with us. He has had a holiday with us; me and another friend went on holiday to Whitby earlier this year. I am so glad that we got to go before this virus invaded our land.

Max still remains our faithful and loving friend, just as Stella was. We could never repay the love and kindness that they have shown to us over the years, but I pray that God will bless Max. I thank God that I got to know the love of such good friends in this life.

I honestly think that not many get to taste the goodness of God in the way that we experienced through this special friendship.

I miss Stella, my best friend, the one who I laughed with and spoke so freely with, the friend who loved me for exactly who I am. It speaks of God's love to me.

A friend loves at all times, and a brother is born for adversity. **(Proverbs 17:17 – NIV)**

A friend is always loyal, and a brother is born to help in time of need. **(Proverbs 17:17 – NLT)**

There are friends that destroy each other, but a real friend sticks closer than a brother. **(Proverbs 18:24 – NLT)**

As we come towards the end of my journey, my story, my thoughts, thank you for sticking with it I hope and pray that you were blessed as you read them. Take care, my friends, and stay safe.

Love Diana

(Originally written on 1st July 2020)

A Dream Come True

I remember back in 2015 a man called John Kiseba came over from Zambia and visited our home. We had supported John in his work for many years, starting the support when we lived in Chorley. Some friends of ours had gone on a mission trip to Zambia and had spent time with John over there. They spoke to us of this man who was full of integrity. John also managed the Refreshed Pot Care House in Kafue, the children's home that I had helped raise the funds to build.

Anyway, John was in the UK doing lots of meetings, with one such gathering at my house. I had prepared an afternoon tea in his honour and I also invited a large group of friends to meet and listen to this inspirational man speak.

When the meeting was drawing to a close, John prayed for me and prayed a blessing on me. I honestly sensed a big blessing coming my way as he prayed.

That was on a Saturday and by the Tuesday my sister was phoning me with some rather amazing news. "How would you like to go to the fjords?"

Are you kidding me? That would be a dream come true, I thought. "Deb, I don't have that kind of money to go there."

"That's ok because I am paying! I have got the most amazing deal – ten nights on a cruise ship with all drinks paid for in the deal. And guess what? It is only £599 each and we will have a balcony."

[40] Debbie in her wheelchair in the fjords © Diana Wood, 2015

I knew the general price of cruises and this was one of the most amazing deals I had ever heard of. I knew that this was the blessing that John had prayed for. I talked to Mick before I said yes. Me and my lovely sister were going on this adventure together. I knew it was a gift for us to spend that special time together, as Deb had been very ill for a long time. We would take her dialysis machine and supplies on board with us. Also, Deb would need to be pushed around in a wheelchair, but it was my joy to do that for her.

We went in June 2015. We sang all the way to Southampton in the car with our '70s music on. The journey went by so quickly. When we arrived at Southampton, we even got the last room in a Premier Inn near to the docks.

When we got on board, we had the most amazing time together. I rediscovered that we both enjoyed entertainment and nice food. When we were kids, Deb and I used to make up our own little musical shows. Every evening, we would go to the restaurant early and then on to a show. This was followed by listening to a live band and dancing. Deb was not well enough to dance, but she would send me off to dance with a group of women on the dance floor. We had such fun and joy together! We loved dressing up to go out of an evening together. Deb said I reminded her of a Barbie doll, which made me laugh as I am a brunette and rounded to say the least.

She said, "It's because you like trying on your clothes until you get it right." It gave her joy to watch me get ready and for us to put our make-up on together.

One evening, a man was doing some kind of comedy juggling act and I literally couldn't stop laughing, even when everyone else had. Deb found this hilarious. Our cruise in the fjords was a time that we treasured in the few years that we had left together.

I cried as we left the ship, trying not to let Deb see me while I was pushing her around in her wheelchair. I knew that we had been given that special time together and it was a dream come true for me to go to the fjords with my beautiful sister.

John Kiseba was to be instrumental in praying for Deb a year later when he came over to the UK yet again.

I truly thank God for that special trip and special time with my sister. I will treasure it for the rest of my days.

Deb went to be with the Lord on 19th February 2019. I still miss her every day!

(Originally written on 1st August 2020)

A Blue Horizon

I remember when we lived back in Chorley in our end-terraced house. The kitchen needed decorating desperately; in fact, we needed a whole new kitchen, but we had no money to get one. It was making me depressed because it looked such a state.

In a moment of madness, I decided that I would strip the wallpaper and decorate it myself. When I had stripped the walls, they were right down to the grey breeze blocks. I said to the Lord, "This is an artistic impression of my life right now," and that is exactly how I felt about my life at that time.

I found some paint called 'blue horizon' and I again spoke to the Lord and said, *I am painting these walls in blue horizon because I am sick of grey days; I need a blue horizon in my life!*

I began to pray for my kitchen to be made new. I painted up a set of shelves in bright colours and had them fixed to the wall. Then I painted an old dresser in the same bright colours. I did what I could do to make things as nice and bright as possible. I still needed some new kitchen units, so I prayed as I usually did when I had done what I could but could go no further.

Mick and I went to an evening meeting at a church that we didn't usually go to. Someone approached me with an envelope which had a cheque for £500 inside it! The woman said, "That is for your kitchen." I had prayed for exactly that amount to finish off my kitchen.

There was a sale on at B&Q and I managed to design my own kitchen and buy the units at half price. A very good friend was a professional kitchen fitter and he put the units in for us free of charge (in fact, the cost was a plate of my Lancashire Hotpot). My kitchen now looked amazing. Bright white units with dark blue worktops, amethyst walls painted over the blue horizon, and a grey and white floor covering. It could have made the pages of any home magazine. It looked great and bright, too.

Mick was studying at university at the same time as we were completing the kitchen. Mick got a totally unexpected gift of money from the university bursary fund to help us with our family's daily living needs. It was a large amount and there was money left over to buy new accessories for the kitchen to finish it all off perfectly!

What an adventure we have when God is in our lives! A famous speaker called Joyce Meyer said, "You do your best and God will do the rest."

As I finish this book, may I encourage you to dare to pray to the Lord in whatever situation that you find yourself in.

Circumstances do not have the final say in our lives, but a God who holds the universe in His hands does!

Thanks for reading my stories of real life and hope in God in the midst of it all!

Love Diana xxx

(Originally written on 2nd August 2020)

About The Author

Diana Wood

Diana Wood has been serving and speaking in women's ministries for over thirty years. Diana has a heart to equip, empower, and encourage all people but especially women. Diana has spent her life collecting broken people like buried treasure and helping them polish the gold until it shines again. Wife to Mick for nearly forty years, mother of five and Nana to six beautiful children.

Printed in Great Britain
by Amazon

64177582R00071